International Trade Centre

Standards and quality management

COMMONWEALTH
SECRETARIAT

Influencing and Meeting International Standards

Challenges for developing countries

*Volume One – Background information,
findings from case studies and technical
assistance needs*

Geneva 2004

ABSTRACT FOR TRADE INFORMATION SERVICES

2004   F-09.35.3
                                                        INF

INTERNATIONAL TRADE CENTRE UNCTAD/WTO
COMMONWEALTH SECRETARIAT
Influencing and Meeting International Standards: Challenges for developing countries
Geneva: ITC/CS, 2004. xiii, 126 p.

Study dealing with technical assistance needs of developing countries in order to conform with technical regulations and sanitary and phytosanitary measures required by export markets – provides background information on the objectives and rules of the Agreement on Technical Barriers to Trade (TBT) and the Agreement on the Application of Sanitary and Phytosanitary Measures (SPS); draws upon experiences of selected developing countries in this area to identify their needs for technical assistance, and to examine the development of standardization and conformity assessment systems in developing countries. (Reprint of 2003 edition)

Subject descriptors: **Conformity Assessment, SPS, Standardization, TBT**.

English, French, Spanish (separate editions)

International Trade Centre, Palais des Nations, 1211 Geneva 10, Switzerland
Commonwealth Secretariat, Marlborough House, London, United Kingdom

Digital image on the cover: © Digital Vision

ITC/P181.E/TSS/BAS/04-XII   ISBN 0-85092-783-8
                                          United Nations Sales No. E.03.III.T.9

Foreword

Trade liberalization is undoubtedly opening up market opportunities for developing countries. Yet many of them, especially the least developed, still have enormous difficulties in making effective use of such openings, whether they result from multilateral agreements or from special arrangements such as the European Union's Everything But Arms initiative or the Africa Growth and Opportunities Act in the United States.

Supply-side problems notwithstanding, meeting the exacting norms and standards of export markets presents a major challenge to developing countries in their quest for world markets. More fundamentally, as the present publication confirms, developing countries currently have little input into the international standards that serve as the basis for technical regulations and sanitary and phytosanitary measures in export markets. They lack both the financial and human resources to play an active role in the deliberations of the relevant international bodies. They also typically lack the infrastructure needed to demonstrate acceptable conformity to the voluntary and mandatory technical requirements in their export markets.

The present publication, based on a sample of case studies, documents these gaps and examines the difficulties hindering the export efforts of developing countries due to shortcomings in their standardization and conformity assessment infrastructure. The publication presents an inventory of the technical assistance needs of developing countries in relation to technical regulations and sanitary and phytosanitary measures.

Needs are enormous and diverse. To address them comprehensively will require strong cooperation across the whole range of development partners. This study by the Commonwealth Secretariat and the International Trade Centre UNCTAD/WTO addresses some of the identified challenges.

Don McKinnon
Secretary General
Commonwealth Secretariat

J. Denis Bélisle
Executive Director
International Trade Centre

Acknowledgements

The publication is the outcome of a project that was jointly funded by the Commonwealth Secretariat and the International Trade Centre (UNCTAD/WTO).

The conclusions drawn and recommendations offered are based on information provided by all those in the six countries in which the case studies were undertaken (Jamaica, Kenya, Malaysia, Mauritius, Namibia and Uganda), who were approached for insights, who gave their time and openly shared their experiences and opinions about improving the capacity of developing countries to meet the standards, technical regulations, and sanitary and phytosanitary measures of export markets. The cooperation extended by representatives of international organizations and the Governments is appreciated. Digby F. Gascoine, Spencer J. Henson, Gene A. Hutchinson, John F. Landos, Samuel A. Mwambazi and Henri J. van Rensberg carried out the case studies.

Vinod Rege, Adviser on WTO Issues to the Commonwealth Secretariat, **Shyam K. Gujadhur**, Senior Adviser on Standards and Quality Management and **Roswitha Franz**, ITC, wrote this publication based on reports submitted by the six consultants.

The effective management and guidance provided by the following individuals contributed to the successful completion of the project:

❑ R. Badrinath, Director, Division of Trade Support Services, ITC;

❑ P. Berthelot, Deputy Director, Special Advisory Services Division, Commonwealth Secretariat;

❑ S. Meitzel, Chief, Business Advisory Services, ITC;

❑ S. Fakahau, Chief Programme Officer, Special Advisory Services Division, Commonwealth Secretariat.

Additional support for research was provided by Caroline Schwaller-Lo Moro, Sebastian Mayr and Matias Urrutigoity.

The book was edited by Alison Southby. Desktop publishing and final copy editing were done by Carmelita Endaya.

Contents

Foreword   iii

Acknowledgements   v

Note   xiii

Introduction   1

    Organization of this publication   4

Overview   5

  General   5

  Summary of background information   5

    Overview of the main provisions of the Agreements on TBT and SPS   5

      Objectives of the two Agreements   5

      Definition of the terms used in the Agreements   6

      Rules governing application   6

      Deviation from the rule on using international standards   7

    Procedures adopted by international standard-setting organizations for formulating
and adopting standards   7

      Organizations engaged in preparing trade-related standards   7

      Overview of international standard-setting organizations   7

        Organizational forms   8

        Pattern of membership   8

        Membership fees   8

      Procedures adopted for technical work on the formulation of standards 8

      Mechanisms used or under consideration in the international standard-setting organizations
for improving participation by developing countries   10

  Main findings in the case studies   11

    Level of participation of developing countries in international standardization activities:
findings and conclusions of the case studies   11

    Experience of developing countries in participation in regional standardization activities 12

    Difficulties encountered in complying with the technical regulations and sanitary and
phytosanitary measures applied by importing countries   13

      Technical regulations   13

      Sanitary and phytosanitary measures   14

Progress made by the case study countries in establishing the administrative mechanisms required for the implementation of the Agreements 14

Administrative arrangements for implementation of the Agreements on TBT and SPS 14

Transparency obligations 15

Enquiry points 15

Notification obligations 15

Progress made in aligning national standards to international standards and basing technical regulations and sanitary and phytosanitary measures on international standards 16

Progress made in accreditation of laboratories, inspection bodies and certification bodies 17

Capacities for ensuring that imported goods conform to TBT regulations and SPS measures 17

Technical assistance: identified needs and suggested delivery mechanism 18

Recommendations and observations in the joint report of the consultants 18

Specific areas for technical assistance 18

Assistance aimed at improving the participation of developing countries in standardization activities at international level 19

Workshops prior to meetings of technical committees 20

Mentoring and twinning arrangements 20

Need to establish a forum to encourage countries to enter into mentoring and twinning arrangements, where feasible, on a South-South basis 20

Main features of the framework to be established for facilitating mentoring and twinning arrangements 21

Creating greater awareness among industry and trade associations of the need for active interest in standardization activities at national and international level 22

Assistance to developing countries in meeting the requirements of technical regulations and of sanitary and phytosanitary measures applied in their export markets 22

Provision of practical assistance 22

Preparation of brochures explaining technical regulations and sanitary and phytosanitary measures applicable to certain products 22

Assistance to interested developing countries for establishing systems to alert exporters to changes in technical regulations or sanitary and phytosanitary measures 23

Assistance for the establishment of accreditation bodies at national and regional level 23

Concluding observations 23

CHAPTER 1

Description of the main features and rules of the Agreements on TBT and SPS

25

General 25

Agreement on Technical Barriers to Trade 26

Definitions of the terms used: standards, technical regulations and conformity assessment procedures 26

Obligations to use international standards 27

Other specific rules 28

Agreement on the Application of Sanitary and Phytosanitary Measures 28

General 28

Definition of sanitary and phytosanitary measures 28

Approach of the Agreement on SPS 30

Main differences between the two Agreements 30

CHAPTER 2

International standard-setting organizations: procedures and practices followed in formulating and adopting standards 33

General 33

Overview of the procedures and practices followed in adopting international standards 34
  General 34
  Organizational forms 34
  Pattern of membership 34
    Who can become a member? 34
    Organizations having only one class of membership 36
    Organizations having different classes of membership 36
  Membership fees 36
    Intergovernmental organizations belonging to the United Nations family 36
    Other intergovernmental and non-governmental organizations 36
  Procedures for the formulation of standards 38
    Procedures adopted for technical work on formulation of standards 38
    Procedures for the adoption of international standards 40

Other measures taken by the international standard-setting bodies to facilitate participation of developing countries 40
    Financial assistance to attend meetings 41
      Payment of a special allowance by the organization 41
      Sponsorship by developed countries 41
      Holding workshops prior to technical committee meetings 41
      Sponsorship under ISO's Development Programme 41
    Submission of comments on draft standards by e-mail 41
    Establishment of special committees or projects 41
    Workshops for improving participation of developing countries 42
    Actions by international organizations for facilitating participation of developing countries through establishment of trust funds 45

CHAPTER 3

Level of participation of developing countries in international standardization activities: findings and conclusions of the case studies 46

General 46

Findings on the level of participation in the activities of the international standard-setting bodies 46
    International standard-setting bodies producing standards used in sanitary and phytosanitary measures 46
    International standard-setting bodies producing standards used in technical regulations 47

Lessons that can be drawn 49

CHAPTER 4

Participation of developing countries in regional standardization activities 51

General 51

Aims and objectives of standardization activities undertaken on a regional basis 51

Problems encountered in participating in regional standardization activities   53

Complementary role played by the regional commissions and committees of the international standard-setting organizations   54

Need for establishment of regional laboratories and regional service and repair centres   54

    Regional laboratories   54

    Regional centres for repair of test equipment   55

CHAPTER 5

Problems experienced by the case study countries in complying with technical regulations and sanitary and phytosanitary measures of importing markets   56

General   56

Water treatment, fumigation and other requirements for control of pests or diseases   58

Problems posed by Maximum Residue Limits (MRLs)   58

Inspection of processing facilities by inspectors from importing countries   58

    Fish and fish products   59

    Ackee   59

    Meat and meat products   59

    Cheese and cheese products   59

Registration and prior clearance requirements   59

Application of standards that are higher than the international standards   60

Problems encountered in trade with other developing countries   60

CHAPTER 6

Progress made in adopting administrative arrangements for the implementation of the Agreements on TBT and SPS and in abiding by their obligations   62

General   62

Administrative arrangements for the implementation of the Agreements on TBT and SPS   62

Transparency obligations   63

    Enquiry points   64

    Notification obligations   64

        Requirement for notification of proposed technical regulations or sanitary and phytosanitary measures   64

        Circulation of notifications received from WTO   65

        Notifications by the case study countries   66

Progress made in aligning national standards to international standards and basing technical regulations or sanitary and phytosanitary measures on international standards   67

    Alignment of national standards to international standards   67

        Industrial products   67

        Agricultural products   68

    Use of international standards in technical regulations and sanitary and phytosanitary measures   68

        Technical regulations   68

        Sanitary and phytosanitary measures   68

Progress made in accreditation of laboratories, inspection bodies and certification bodies   69

Capacities for ensuring that imported goods conform to regulations and measures   69

CHAPTER 7

Technical assistance: identified needs and suggested delivery mechanism

70

Recommendations and observations in the joint report of the consultants   70

Specific areas in which technical assistance is needed   71

General   71

Assistance aimed at improving the participation of developing countries in standardization activities at international level   72

Workshops prior to meetings of technical committees   73

Mentoring and twinning arrangements: their objectives and purpose   74

Need to establish a forum to encourage countries to enter into mentoring and twinning arrangements, where feasible, on a South-South basis   74

Main features of the framework to be established for facilitation of mentoring and twinning arrangements   75

Techniques and modalities for promoting dialogue between mentors and twinning countries   76

Creating greater awareness among industry and trade associations of the need to take more active interest in standardization activities at national and international level   77

Assistance to developing countries in meeting the requirements of technical regulations and of sanitary and phytosanitary measures applied in their export markets   78

Provision of practical assistance   78

Preparation of brochures explaining technical regulations and sanitary and phytosanitary measures applicable to certain products   78

Assistance to interested developing countries for establishing systems to alert exporters to changes in technical regulations or sanitary and phytosanitary measures   79

Assistance for the establishment of accreditation bodies at national and regional level   80

Concluding observations   80

Appendices

I.   Extracts from general comments about technical assistance made by the six consultants based on the twelve case studies   83

II.   Agreement on Technical Barriers to Trade   96

III.   Agreement on the Application of Sanitary and Phytosanitary Measures   115

Boxes

1.   Terms of reference for the case studies   3

2.   Illustrative list of import products subject to technical regulations and sanitary and phytosanitary measures   25

3.   Distinction between technical regulations and sanitary and phytosanitary measures: Some examples   29

4.   Guidelines for assessment of risk and determination of the appropriate level of sanitary and phytosanitary protection   32

5.   International standard-setting organizations   35

6.   Membership fees   37

7.   Workshop on technical assistance and special and differential treatment in the context of the Agreement on TBT, held by the Committee on TBT in Geneva, July 2000   42

8. ISO General Assembly Workshop on 'Participation of Developing Countries in International Standardization' in Stockholm, September 2002   43

9. Workshop on technical assistance and capacity building related to the Agreement on SPS, held by the Committee on SPS in Geneva, November 2002   44

10. FAO/WHO Trust Fund   45

11. Standards and Trade Development Facility (STDF)   45

12. Regional standard-setting organizations   52

13. Problems experienced by case study countries due to the application of sanitary and phytosanitary measures by importing region/country   57

14. Agencies designated as enquiry points   65

15. Authorities responsible for making notifications to WTO under the Agreements on TBT and SPS   66

16. Strengths and weaknesses of the mechanisms under consideration in international standardization and other organizations for improving developing country participation in the standard-setting process   73

17. Basic information needed for promoting dialogue between countries who could act as mentors and those needing assistance   77

Note

The following abbreviations are used:

CAC	Codex Alimentarius Commission
CASCO	ISO Committee on Conformity Assessment
CROSQ	CARICOM Regional Organisation for Standards and Quality
DEVCO	ISO Committee on Developing Country Matters
DEVPRO	ISO Programme for the Developing Countries
EU	European Union
FAO	Food and Agriculture Organization of the United Nations
GATT	General Agreement on Tariffs and Trade
GNP	Gross national product
ICT	Information and Communication Technology
IEC	International Electrotechnical Commission
IPPC	International Plant Protection Convention
ISO	International Organization for Standardization
ISSOs	International standard-setting organizations
ITC	International Trade Centre
ITU	International Telecommunication Union
ITU-D	ITU Telecommunication Development Sector
ITU-R	ITU Radiocommunication Sector
ITU-T	ITU Telecommunication Standardization
LDCs	Least developed countries
MFN	Most favoured nation
MRLs	Maximum residue limits
OIE	Office International des Epizooties
OIML	International Organization of Legal Metrology
SADC	Southern African Development Community
SC	Sub-Committee
SIRIM	Standards and Industrial Research Institute of Malaysia
SPS	(Agreement on) Sanitary and Phytosanitary Measures
SwF	Swiss franc
TBT	(Agreement on) Technical Barriers to Trade
TC	Technical Committee
UNCTAD	United Nations Conference on Trade and Development
USAID	United States Agency for International Development
WHO	World Health Organization
WTO	World Trade Organization

Introduction

All countries require imported goods to conform to the technical regulations that they apply to domestically produced products for health, safety and consumer protection. Imported agricultural products also have to conform to sanitary and phytosanitary measures which are applied to protect human or animal life from food-borne risks and from plant-carried diseases. Though these regulations and measures are applied by governments for legitimate policy reasons, they could in practice create barriers to trade. Such barriers arise if regulations differ from country to country. Exporting firms have to ensure in such situations that the products they export meet the differing requirements. This adds to their costs.

The WTO Agreement on Technical Barriers to Trade (TBT) and the Agreement on the Application of Sanitary and Phytosanitary Measures (SPS) therefore specify that countries should base their technical regulations and sanitary and phytosanitary measures on international standards. The two Agreements also specify that there shall be presumption that such regulations and measures do not cause barriers to trade if they are based on international standards. Countries may introduce or maintain sanitary or phytosanitary measures which result in a higher level of sanitary or phytosanitary protection than would be achieved by measures based on the relevant international standards, guidelines or recommendations if, for instance, there is a scientific justification. Countries do not have to base their technical regulations on international standards if there are fundamental climatic or geographic factors that justify the use of different standards.

To ensure that international standards are used to the maximum extent possible by countries in adopting their technical regulations and sanitary and phytosanitary measures, the two Agreements urge countries to 'play a full part, within the limits of their resources' in the preparation by international standard-setting bodies of international standards for products for which they have either adopted or expect to adopt such technical regulations or sanitary and phytosanitary measures.

Even though these two Agreements thus place an obligation on members to use international standards in their technical regulations and sanitary and phytosanitary measures and call on them to take an active part in international standardization activities, only a few developing countries are able today to participate in work on developing standards at international level. The participation of this limited number of countries is also in most cases not effective, as it is not supported by the background research and analysis that are required to ensure that technical specifications of the products they produce and processes used in the manufacture of such products are adequately taken into account in developing international standards.

The inability of a large number of developing countries to participate effectively in international standardization activities poses serious actual and potential problems to the trade of these countries. If an importing country uses international standards in its technical regulations and sanitary and phytosanitary measures, exporting enterprises from developing countries would have to change their own standards to bring them into conformity with such mandatory regulations if the product specifications in the standards they use are not reflected in international standards because of their non-participation. Otherwise, they would not be able to export their products to that country.

Moreover, since compliance with requirements laid down by technical regulations and sanitary and phytosanitary measures is mandatory, countries often require imported products to be accompanied by certificates issued by properly accredited third party conformity assessment bodies or, more typically in the case of sanitary and phytosanitary measures, certification by official bodies in the exporting country. In most developing countries the infrastructure which is required for certification of conformity to standards has not yet been fully developed. The result is that importing countries often insist on post-arrival examination of the product after importation, or resort to systems of prior inspection and approval of the products in the exporting country by their officials. These requirements not only add to the costs of exporters but also in some cases lead to delays.

Against this background, it was considered that developing countries need technical assistance to:

❑ Overcome the problems they encounter in participating effectively in international standardization activities;

❑ Meet effectively the technical requirements in their export markets; and

❑ Build capacities for deriving full benefits from the WTO Agreements on TBT and SPS.

In order to identify these technical assistance needs, the Commonwealth Secretariat and the International Trade Centre decided jointly to undertake case studies in six countries.[1]

In selecting countries for the case studies, the existence of a gap in the extent to which standardization and conformity assessment systems are developed in different developing countries was taken into account by studying the experience in developing countries at various stages of development.

Among the countries selected for the study, Malaysia is considered as a developing country with relatively more developed national institutions engaged in standardization and conformity activities. Jamaica, Kenya, Mauritius and Uganda have been able to make some progress in work on standardization and conformity assessment by establishing national standard-setting and conformity assessment bodies, while Namibia represented countries whose experience at national level in the area of standardization and conformity assessment are at a nascent stage.

It should be noted that the basis on which countries were selected is for analytical purposes only, to assess broadly the technical assistance needs of developing countries at widely different stages of development. It should not be interpreted as involving any value judgement on the actual level of development in standardization activities in each of these countries.

Box 1 contains the terms of reference that were used for the preparation of the case studies.

---

1   Case studies were carried out in the latter half of 2001.

Box 1
Terms of reference for the case studies

i)   To assess the extent to which the country is able and willing to participate effectively in international standard-setting organizations preparing standards used by countries in adopting technical regulations and sanitary and phytosanitary measures;

ii)   To examine the extent and nature of infrastructure in the country relating to standardization and regulatory activities and conformity assessment at the national level, and participation in international standard-setting organizations relating to SPS and TBT measures;

iii) To identify the major constraints limiting the effective participation of the country in international standard-setting organizations relating to SPS and TBT measures;

iv)   To examine the problems and difficulties faced by the country due to technical regulations, conformity assessment practices and sanitary and phytosanitary measures in its main export markets, both with respect to compliance and conformity assessment, relating these problems to the need for appropriate international standards where appropriate; and

v)   To examine the need of the country for assistance for, inter alia:

❑ Further development of activities for developing and adopting standards for products of export interest;

❑ Developing technical regulations and sanitary and phytosanitary measures based on international standards;

❑ Creating greater awareness among industries (producing both goods and services) and their associations of the need to undertake background research and analytical work that is necessary for their effective participation in standardization activities at national level;

❑ Assisting the national standard-setting body and/or the government in participating in the work at international level on developing international standards, taking into account the existing rules, procedures and practices adopted by the international standard-setting bodies (e.g. ISO and CAC) in formulating and establishing international standards, and the steps which the international standard-setting bodies are taking for facilitating improved and effective participation of developing countries in the development of such standards; and

❑ Developing and strengthening national infrastructures for demonstrating compliance with technical regulations and sanitary and phytosanitary measures in export markets.

The studies for each country in the area of technical regulations and SPS measures were undertaken separately by experts with specialized knowledge in the subject area.

Organization of this publication

The whole publication is divided into two volumes. This first volume contains background information, findings from case studies and technical assistance needs.

Volume two is divided into three parts:

❑ Part One: Notes on procedures followed by selected international standard-setting organizations (ISSOs) and on international accreditation bodies.

❑ Part Two: Country reports on technical barriers to trade (TBT).

❑ Part Three: Country reports on sanitary and phytosanitary (SPS) measures.

Volume two contains background information that would be useful in appreciating the points made and views expressed in volume one.

Overview

General

This overview is divided into three parts:

❑ *Summary of the background information;*

❑ *Main findings in the case studies; and*

❑ *Technical assistance.*

The first part provides background information on the objectives and rules of the Agreements on TBT and SPS and of the procedures adopted by international standard-setting organizations in formulating draft standards and in adopting them as international standards.

The second part highlights the main findings in the case studies which relate to:

❑ *The level of participation of developing countries in international standardization activities;*

❑ *Their experience of participation in regional standardization activities;*

❑ *Difficulties encountered by them in complying with technical regulations and SPS measures; and*

❑ *Progress made by them in establishing the administrative mechanisms required for the implementation of the Agreements and for compliance with the obligations which they impose.*

The third part outlines the technical assistance needs identified from the case studies and a suggested mechanism for the delivery of technical assistance.

Summary of background information

Overview of the main provisions of the Agreements on TBT and SPS

Objectives of the two Agreements

International rules governing the application of technical regulations are contained in the Agreement on Technical Barriers to Trade (TBT). The Agreement on the Application of Sanitary and Phytosanitary Measures (SPS) lays down rules which countries must abide by in applying such measures.

The basic aim of the detailed rules and guidelines laid down by the two Agreements is to ensure that technical regulations and sanitary and phytosanitary measures are not formulated and applied by countries in order to create arbitrary obstacles to trade. The Agreements envisage that this could be attained if countries use, wherever appropriate and possible, international standards in formulating their technical regulations and sanitary and phytosanitary measures, or in developing national standards. Likewise, the Agreements call on them to use guidelines and recommendations developed by the international standard-setting organizations as a basis for their conformity assessment procedures.

To provide an incentive for countries to use international standards, the two Agreements provide that 'where international standards, guides or recommendations' have been used as a basis for technical regulations, sanitary and phytosanitary measures and their related conformity assessment procedures, it shall be presumed that they do not create unnecessary obstacles to trade. The Agreements further urge member countries to participate in the work of the international standard-setting organizations, so that international standards will be available for products for which they wish to adopt technical regulations or sanitary and phytosanitary measures, or develop standards. Countries are also urged to participate in the activities of such organizations in order to develop international guidelines and recommendations that can be used in developing national conformity assessment procedures.

Definition of the terms used in the Agreements

Technical regulations cover, among other things, product specifications which lay down the characteristics of products, their quality and safety, and processes and methods used in production, if such production methods have an effect on quality. Such regulations are applied by countries to both industrial and agricultural products.

These regulations need to be distinguished from sanitary and phytosanitary measures, which are applied only to agricultural products. The term 'sanitary measures' is used to cover regulations that lay down food safety specifications or specifications aimed at preventing food-borne pests or diseases entering into a country. Where the objective of the specification is to ensure that imported plant varieties do not bring in plant-borne pests or diseases, it is called a 'phytosanitary measure'.

Conformity assessment procedures are used, directly or indirectly, to determine that relevant requirements in technical regulations or standards are fulfilled, including procedures for: sampling, testing and inspection; evaluation, verification and assurance of conformity; registration, accreditation and approval; and combinations of these.

Control, inspection and approval procedures check and ensure the fulfilment of sanitary and phytosanitary measures. Those procedures include procedures for sampling, testing and certification.

Rules governing application

Compliance with technical regulations and sanitary and phytosanitary measures is mandatory. Both domestically produced and imported products must fully conform to the requirements which they lay down.

The technical regulations are further to be applied to imported products on a most-favoured-nation (MFN) basis. The Agreement on SPS specifies that, in the case of sanitary and phytosanitary measures, the obligation to apply MFN treatment is also generally applicable. However, where the objective of the measure is to prevent pests or diseases not present in the country from being brought into the country, it is open to a country to deviate from the MFN rule and to apply the measures only to products imported from countries where such pests or diseases exist.

Deviation from the rule on using international standards

The rules of the Agreements on TBT and SPS permit countries to deviate in certain situations from the obligation they impose to use international standards in formulating and adopting technical regulations and sanitary and phytosanitary measures. There are, however, differences in the conditions under which such deviations are permitted. Under the Agreement on TBT a country may adopt a technical regulation which prescribes requirements that are different or higher than those in existing international standards only where it is considered necessary because of fundamental climatic or geographical factors or for technological considerations. The Agreement on SPS, on the other hand, gives the right to a country to introduce sanitary and phytosanitary measures that are higher than international standards, if there is a scientific justification and if it is established, on the basis of assessment of risks, that a more stringent measure is needed in order to achieve the appropriate level of protection.

Procedures adopted by international standard-setting organizations for formulating and adopting standards

Organizations engaged in preparing trade-related standards

There are at present over 50 international standard-setting organizations (ISSOs) engaged in developing international standards. However, only a few of them develop standards that are trade-related. The Agreement on SPS specifies that the obligations which it imposes apply to international standards developed, in particular, by the following three international standardization organizations:

❏ Codex Alimentarius Commission (CAC);
❏ Office International des Epizooties (OIE);
❏ International Plant Protection Convention (IPPC).

The Agreement on TBT, on the other hand, does not specify any international standardizing body; it is, however, generally recognized that its rules requiring countries to use international standards in formulating and adopting technical regulations apply to standards developed by:

❏ International Organization for Standardization (ISO);[2]
❏ International Electrotechnical Commission (IEC);
❏ International Telecommunication Union (ITU);
❏ International Organization of Legal Metrology (OIML).[3]

Overview of international standard-setting organizations

The seven organizations mentioned vary considerably in their:

❏ Organizational forms;
❏ Patterns of membership, and
❏ Criteria used for determining membership fees.

---

2   The short form, ISO, is the same in all languages. It is derived from the Greek word *isos*, meaning 'equal'.
3   The abbreviation is based on the French name: Organisation internationale de métrologie légale.

Organizational forms

Of the three main organizations, which are responsible for the formulation of standards that could be used in sanitary and phytosanitary measures, two are intergovernmental organizations belonging to the United Nations family. CAC is jointly managed by FAO and WHO; FAO also provides the secretariat for IPPC. OIE is an intergovernmental organization, but it does not belong to the United Nations family.

Of the four international organizations which formulate standards used in technical regulations, two – ISO and IEC – are non-governmental organizations. Most international standards for industrial products are formulated by these two organizations. Of the remaining two, ITU is an intergovernmental organization belonging to the United Nations family. Although OIML is also an intergovernmental organization, it does not belong to the United Nations family.

Pattern of membership

The pattern of membership shows also some variations. In the intergovernmental organizations belonging to the United Nations family which are engaged in standardization work – ITU, CAC and IPPC – and in OIE, members have the same status. All of them have a right to participate in all aspects of the ongoing work and have a right to vote. The situation is different in the case of organizations such as ISO, IEC and OIML, which have full membership as well as other classes of membership, such as correspondent, associate or subscriber members. These other classes of membership have been created by these organizations to create awareness of the importance of their work among countries that are not in a position to become full members, and to prepare those countries gradually for full membership by familiarizing them with their work. These members have either no rights or restricted rights for participation in the technical work relating to the formulation of international standards and do not have the right to vote.

Membership fees

The financial contribution that member countries have to make to the budgets also varies from organization to organization. Member countries do not pay separate fees for standardization work done by standard-setting organizations belonging to the United Nations family. On the other hand, member countries have to pay separate fees for membership of intergovernmental organizations that do not belong to the United Nations family (e.g. OIML and OIE) and non-governmental organizations (ISO and IEC). However, all these organizations, except OIML, use criteria that result in developing countries paying lower fees than those charged to developed countries. OIML's criteria are based on the size of the population.

Procedures adopted for technical work on the formulation of standards

The procedures adopted by these organizations for work at a technical level on the formulation of standards also show marked variations. Each organization's procedure is greatly influenced by the practices it has followed in the past and by the framework it has adopted for decision-making on administrative and on technical matters.

In the case of international standard-setting organizations belonging to the United Nations family, the procedures used for work in the standardization field are also influenced by the practices they follow for work in other areas.

There are, however, a few principles and elements which are common to all of these organizations. These are described below:

❑ The decision to commence work on a new standard is taken by the relevant body within the organization that is responsible for making such decisions, at the request of a member or a group of members, or on an initiative taken by the secretariat.

❑ Once the decision is taken and the definition and technical scope of the standard are agreed upon, the responsibility for 'negotiating technical specifications' and 'consensus building' on the draft standard is assigned, in the case of:

   – ISO, IEC and OIML, to technical committees and sub-committees;
   – ITU, to study groups;
   – CAC, to general subject or commodity committees or to ad hoc intergovernmental task forces;
   – OIE, to one of the specialist commissions; and
   – IPPC, to working groups.

❑ The draft standard prepared in discussions and negotiations at expert level is circulated by the secretariat to all members for comments and views.

❑ The comments received from members are passed on for review and examination to the relevant committees or commissions.

❑ The final draft is prepared by the committees or commissions, after taking into account the comments received from members.

❑ It is then transmitted to the apex body of the organization (CAC, OIE, IPPC), or the relevant committee (OIML), or full members (ISO, IEC) for its adoption as an international standard.

It is important to note, however, that there are also considerable differences between the seven organizations in the way in which the technical work on the formulation of standards is undertaken by the technical committees and commissions.

In the case of ISO and IEC, once the decision to assign the work to a technical committee is taken, the major responsibility for providing chairmanship, secretarial and technical support devolves on the member country which agrees to provide host facilities for undertaking such work. In CAC the work is given to a general subject or commodity committee or to an ad hoc intergovernmental task force which is hosted by a member country. The country providing host facilities also agrees to meet all expenditure relating to such work. The adoption by these organizations of decentralized systems for undertaking technical work at different places and away from the headquarters of the organizations has been necessitated both by the volume of their work and the constraints put on them by the availability of financial resources. These three organizations are responsible for over 85 per cent of the trade-related standards developed every year.

On the other hand, secretariats of organizations such as IPPC, ITU and OIE, whose mandate covers only a limited range of product areas, are able to produce best results by arranging expert level meetings directly under the umbrella of their secretariats and meeting the cost of such work from their budgets.

The decentralized system adopted by ISO, IEC and CAC does suffer from some limitations. The host country is best placed to show leadership in a specialist committee, and this gives it both prestige and influence. Most developing countries do not possess the scientific personnel required for providing secretariat assistance and for supporting research facilities. Some developing countries that have the expert human resources cannot make a bid for securing host facilities, as they lack the financial resources needed to meet the costs of such work. The result is that, in 2001, developed countries held about 90 per cent of the technical committees and sub-committees established by ISO, IEC and CAC.

Mechanisms used or under consideration in the international standard-setting organizations for improving participation by developing countries

All of these organizations are at present using or considering using a variety of mechanisms aimed at facilitating participation by developing countries in their work. These include:

❑ Having developing countries act as co-host of secretariats to technical committees or commissions, and their officials as co-chairpersons.

❑ Financial assistance to attend meetings through:

  – Payment of allowances by the organization to delegations attending the meeting to cover travel costs and other related expenditure.

  – Holding workshops under technical assistance programmes before the meetings of the apex bodies of technical commissions or committees, to enable participants to stay on and participate in the meetings.

  – Encouraging developed countries to sponsor participation by countries having a trade interest in the product for which standards are being formulated, by agreeing to meet travel and other related expenditure from their bilateral assistance programmes.

  – Sponsorship under development programmes for officers from developing countries to attend technical meetings.

❑ Permitting member countries to submit comments on draft standards by e-mail.

❑ Establishment of special committees and projects for discussing the problems faced by developing countries in participating in the work of the organization.

In addition, guidelines and principles that should be followed by international standard-setting organizations in formulating standards that are used in technical regulations were laid down in the second triennial review of the Committee on TBT. Solutions to the problems faced by developing countries for participating in standardization activities have been identified:

❑ In the workshop on the technical assistance needs of developing countries related to the Agreement on TBT, organized by the Committee on TBT in July 2000;

❑ In the workshop on 'Enhancing the Participation of Developing Countries in International Standardization', organized by ISO in September 2002; and

❑ In the workshop on technical assistance and capacity building related to the Agreement on SPS, organized by the Committee on SPS in November 2002.

The recommendations adopted at the TBT workshop envisage the adoption of a programme by developed countries for providing technical assistance 'to improve expertise through, *inter alia*, making experts available to them', 'South-South cooperation by sharing information' and 'encouragement of mentoring and twinning arrangements'. As regards the recommendations made by the ISO workshop, the ISO General Assembly, which considered them, has requested the ISO Council 'to accelerate the implementation of the concept of twinning arrangements as a means of building capacity and the use of ICT (electronic communication) to facilitate participation in the international standardization activities'. One conclusion emerging from the SPS workshop was that the review and updating of the legal framework for sanitary and phytosanitary measures was an extremely important obstacle to implementing sanitary and phytosanitary measures in developing countries.

International organizations such as the World Bank and WTO have taken measures recently to establish trust funds that will facilitate attendance at the meetings and enhance capacities of countries in the work of international standard-setting organizations dealing with sanitary and phytosanitary measures. These measures further complement actions that are being taken by international standard-setting bodies to improve participation by developing countries in international standardization activities.

Main findings in the case studies

This section briefly describes the main findings in the case studies in relation to:

❏ The level of participation of developing countries in international standardization activities: findings and conclusions of the case studies;

❏ Developing countries' experience of participation in regional standardization activities;

❏ Difficulties encountered by them in complying with technical regulations and sanitary and phytosanitary measures; and

❏ Progress made by the case study countries in establishing the administrative mechanisms required for the implementation of the Agreements and for compliance with the obligations which they impose.

Level of participation of developing countries in international standardization activities: findings and conclusions of the case studies

It is clear that conscious efforts are being made by international standard-setting organizations to facilitate the participation of developing countries in all aspects of their work. The question which arises is how far the measures taken have in practice resulted in greater and improved participation by developing countries as a group. One of the major aims of the case studies was to examine this question in light of the practical experience of the selected countries, in order to gain greater insight into the technical assistance that is needed to ensure continued and effective participation of developing countries in these activities.

In carrying out the case studies, it was recognized that the capacity of countries to participate in international standardization activities is greatly influenced by the progress made at national level in developing the infrastructure and institutional framework that are necessary for the development of activities relating to standardization and conformity assessment. Of the countries in the case studies, Malaysia was seen to have better-developed 'institutions engaged in standardization and conformity assessment activities'; Mauritius, Jamaica, Uganda and Kenya have made some progress; and Namibia's development is still at a nascent stage.

The case studies contain a detailed analysis on the extent to which the countries in the case studies have been able to participate in the work of each of the seven international standard-setting bodies. The main conclusions that can be drawn from the analysis in the case studies are listed below.

❑ First, countries like Malaysia are, for the most part, able today to participate in the work at all levels in the international standard-setting organizations in which they have an interest, taking into account the composition of their exports and imports. The participation of countries such as Mauritius, Jamaica, Uganda and Kenya and the lesser-developed countries is, however, generally confined to attending the meetings of the apex bodies of these organizations. In most cases they are not able to attend the meetings of the working groups, sub-committees or technical committees, where work is undertaken at technical level on the formulation of standards for products of trade interest to them, because of financial and other constraints.

❑ Second, except for countries like Malaysia, most of the countries in the study do not appear to have the expertise that is required for participation in the work at technical level on the formulation of standards. Even Malaysia, which has been participating actively in the technical work on formulating standards for products in which it has a trade interest, has not been able to participate in the Codex Committee on Veterinary Drugs, because of 'lack of expertise in setting MRLs and assessing the value of different levels in terms of risk to human health'.

❑ Third, participation in standardization activities, particularly at technical level, is greatly facilitated if the industry and interested business firms assist the agencies responsible for participating in the technical work, by carrying out background research and analytical work. In most developed countries, the main responsibility for undertaking such research and for writing draft standards is taken by the interested industry. The industry also bears the cost of research. For the majority of the countries in the study, one of the important tasks to be addressed is how to create greater awareness among industry and trade groups of the need on their part to carry out the basic research and analytical work that is necessary for participation in the technical work on standardization at international level.

These considerations highlight the need for actions taken by the international standard-setting bodies to improve procedures adopted by them with a view to facilitating participation of developing countries in their work to be complemented by action at national level. Further, it would be unrealistic to expect all developing countries to be able to participate in the technical work on formulation of standards for products of interest to them even if the travel and other costs of officials are met by the international standard-setting organization or through the establishment of trust funds. Almost all countries in the study do not have the capacities to influence the outcome of discussions at technical level in international standard-setting bodies because in most cases they do not have capacities to develop the analytical research data required to support their points of view.

Experience of developing countries in participation in regional standardization activities

The increasing emphasis which developing countries are giving to regional trade and economic cooperation has also resulted in greater attention being paid to work on standardization on a regional basis. This work constitutes an integral part of the measures taken by them for the promotion of intraregional trade.

As a general principle, standards are harmonized by regional standard-setting organizations on the basis of standards adopted at international level by organizations such as ISO, IEC and CAC.

The harmonization of standards on a regional basis expedites the process of aligning national standards to international standards. Regional standards that are not based on international standards are developed only for those agricultural and industrial products which are of importance in intraregional trade and for which international standards either have not been developed or are not likely to be developed because they are of minor importance in international trade.

In the area of sanitary and phytosanitary measures the work undertaken on a regional basis aims at:

❑ Encouraging cooperation among countries for control of pests and other diseases prevailing in the region;

❑ Harmonizing sanitary and phytosanitary measures at regional level; and

❑ Developing environmentally friendly crop protection measures.

The case studies highlight that although countries like Malaysia are able to participate in the work of the regional standard-setting organizations, most of the case study countries encounter problems similar to those they face in participating in international standardization activities.

The lack of expertise on the part of officials participating in the meetings constitutes a major handicap. These difficulties are further accentuated as officials are not able to involve industry, the business community and other stakeholders in the preparatory work needed at national level for participation in the work at technical level. In addition, most of the regional organizations are poorly resourced, and often lack basic administrative support.[4]

However, countries appear to have overcome some of these problems. Work on regional harmonization of standards has been successfully initiated in SADC. A number of regional standards within the East African Community (Kenya, the United Republic of Tanzania and Uganda) have been notified to other WTO Members. CROSQ is making progress in the area of trade facilitation through promotion of development and harmonization of standards, including metrology, technical regulations and mutual recognition of conformity assessment procedures.

The international standard-setting organizations, such as CAC, OIE and IPPC, are actively complementing the work that is being done by the regional standardization bodies through their regional committees or commissions. Participation in the activities of these regional commissions or committees and in the activities of the regional standard-setting organizations would improve the knowledge base of the participating officials and so enhance their capacities for participation in international standardization activities. Continued and effective participation in regional activities may also gradually prepare countries with a trade interest in a product or a product group to participate more effectively in technical work on formulation of standards at international level.

Difficulties encountered in complying with the technical regulations and sanitary and phytosanitary measures applied by importing countries

One of the other aims of the case studies was to assess the difficulties encountered in complying with the technical regulations and sanitary and phytosanitary measures applied in importing countries.

Technical regulations

In the area of technical regulations, by and large, the covered countries appear not to have encountered any serious problems in complying with regulations laying down quality and safety requirements, as these apply to a narrow range

---

4   Henson et al, *Impact of sanitary and phytosanitary measures on developing countries* p. 34.

of industrial products of which they are at present mainly importers and not exporters. Some of these countries, however, appear to be encountering problems in coping with the labelling requirements for food and other consumer products which are being increasingly adopted by developed countries to protect the health of consumers and guard against deceptive practices.

Sanitary and phytosanitary measures

All the case study countries are facing problems in complying with sanitary and phytosanitary measures. The products affected include fresh fruits and vegetables, fish and fish products, meat and meat products, milk and dairy products, and other food products.

The measures that pose difficulties in ensuring compliance and result in some cases in additional costs for exporters can be grouped into five categories:

❑ Water treatment and fumigation requirements for fresh fruits and vegetables for control of pests and diseases;

❑ Problems in complying with maximum residue limits (MRLs) of pesticides and other residues in fresh fruits and vegetables and other food products;

❑ Requirements imposed by certain importing countries that production facilities for fish and fish products and meat and meat products must be inspected and approved by their inspectors or by the local competent authority, as a precondition for allowing imports;

❑ Product registration and pre-clearance requirements; and

❑ Application of technical requirements which are higher than those in international standards.

Illustrations of the difficulties encountered by the case study countries as a result of these requirements are provided in chapter 5.

Progress made by the case study countries in establishing the administrative mechanisms required for the implementation of the Agreements

The case studies also examined the progress made in the implementation of the provisions of the two Agreements.

Administrative arrangements for implementation of the Agreements on TBT and SPS

In all six countries covered by the case studies, the ministry handling WTO-related work is also responsible for coordinating work relating to the implementation of the Agreements on TBT and SPS. The approach adopted by the focal ministry in each country for coordinating the work relating to these Agreements among different ministries shows some variations, however.

The consultants did not have time to assess how far the institutional mechanisms that have been established are effective in securing the involvement of all stakeholders in developing policies to be followed in the discussions at international level on trade-related standardization issues. The general impression provided by the case studies is that, except in the case of Malaysia, there is a considerable need for improvement in the coordination of work among different ministries. In the area of sanitary and phytosanitary measures, for instance, in a number of these countries, the responsibility for work is often fragmented among ministries of health, agriculture and the departments responsible for animal husbandry and veterinary control. It is also important to note, in this context, that while an appropriate institutional framework is essential, the level and effectiveness of coordination depends largely on the willingness of officials from different ministries to share responsibilities. If such willingness does not exist, efforts made in improving and strengthening the institutional mechanism do not produce desired results.

A related issue is of effectiveness of the non-governmental participation in these coordination meetings. Even though the representatives of trade and industry participate in the meetings that are arranged, their contribution in the discussions is often limited, either because of the lack of awareness on their part of the objectives and of the rules of the two Agreements or of the important role which international standards play in facilitating international trade.

Transparency obligations

In order to ensure transparency of technical regulations and sanitary and phytosanitary measures which are being applied or under preparation, the two Agreements impose on the member countries obligations to:

❑ Establish enquiry points; and

❑ Notify to the WTO Secretariat products for which new technical regulations or sanitary and phytosanitary measures are being formulated, immediately after they are available at national level in draft form for comments from the public, if they are not based on international standards and may affect trade.

Enquiry points

All the countries covered by the case studies have established enquiry points to provide information on technical regulations and on sanitary and phytosanitary measures and conformity assessment procedures used in the country, and on national and regional standards.

The enquiry points in most of the case study countries appear to be working reasonably well and are able to meet promptly and effectively the requests for information from interested exporters and importers as well as to respond to the questions received from the governments of the member countries. In the case of countries where the standardization infrastructure is at the nascent stage, financial constraints appear to inhibit the government in allocating fully budgetary resources required for effective operation of the enquiry points.

Notification obligations

The Agreements on TBT and SPS require countries to notify to the WTO Secretariat technical regulations, sanitary and phytosanitary measures and procedures for conformity assessment that they propose to adopt, in all cases where they are not based on international standards and may have an effect on international trade. Such notifications are to be made as soon as the drafts are published for comments and at least two months before their application on a mandatory basis. The purpose of the notification system is to bring the drafts to the attention of other member countries, and through them their industry and business associations, and to give them an opportunity to comment on the drafts, to ensure that the product specifications applied and the process and production methods used in their territories are adequately taken into account by the notifying country in adopting final technical regulations or sanitary and phytosanitary measures.

The extent to which countries covered by the case studies have been able to take advantage of the notification procedures for commenting on the drafts of regulations and measures circulated under the system appears, however, to be limited. This could be attributed to two factors.

First, with the increasing attention being paid in most countries, particularly developed countries, to protection in consumer interests and to food safety, the number of notifications being circulated by WTO for comments is on the increase. Second, because of resource constraints and lack of expertise, it is difficult to sort out the notifications and circulate them to interested parties.

As regards the obligations that these rules impose on developing countries, all the case study countries have designated authorities that are responsible for notifying to WTO their proposed technical regulations and sanitary and phytosanitary measures not based on international standards and which may affect trade. These authorities are also responsible for notifying to WTO emergency measures taken to restrict or prohibit imports on health and sanitary grounds.

Many of the case study countries appear to have established procedures requiring ministries and regulatory authorities to transmit the draft regulations or measures to the designated authorities, so that the authorities can transmit them to the WTO Secretariat for circulation to all member countries. However, the actual number of notifications made to WTO by most of these countries is small, particularly in the area of technical regulations, and may not cover all the regulations that are being adopted. In several case study countries a number of standards have been made mandatory. These have become technical regulations but were not notified to WTO. More notifications appear to have been made to WTO of SPS measures; the majority of them are, however, emergency measures to restrict or prohibit imports.

Progress made in aligning national standards to international standards and basing technical regulations and sanitary and phytosanitary measures on international standards

One of the aims of the Agreements on TBT and SPS is to encourage countries to ensure that the mandatory and voluntary technical requirements adopted by them do not constitute barriers to trade, by aligning them to international standards. The question arises of how far developing countries have been able to align their technical regulations, sanitary and phytosanitary measures and national standards to international standards.

A recent study[5] by ISO on the problems faced 'by the standardization bodies and other stakeholders from developing countries' has found that, in 70 per cent of the countries, less than 50 per cent of the national standards were identical to international standards. In the remaining developing countries covered by the study, the percentage was significantly lower.

According to the study, the main reason for the reluctance of these countries to pursue work on the alignment of their national standards to international standards is that they have not been able to participate in the work on formulating the relevant international standards. They therefore remain unsure of the extent to which international standards are suitable for use by their industries.

The study also mentions other reasons for such reluctance, such as lack of funds at the level of national standard-setting bodies and the industry, lack of awareness on their part of the need for such alignment, and lack of expertise in standardization. These findings in the ISO study are further confirmed by the case studies.

---

5   Participation of developing countries in international standardization: Background paper presented to ISO General Assembly Workshop, Stockholm, 24 September 2002 (page 21).

The ISO study covers broadly the standards prepared by it, which apply largely to industrial products. The situation in relation to standards applied to agricultural products, however, appears to be different. In most countries the national standards, both voluntary and mandatory, applied to food products appear to be based on Codex standards.

A related question is how far the technical regulations that these countries adopt are based on international standards. According to the ISO study referred to above, in 61 per cent of the countries covered by the study, more than half of the mandatory regulations were not based on international standards. What is further revealing is that, in 59 per cent of these countries, more than half of the technical regulations were not even based on national standards. The study attributes this to the lack of cooperation between standardizing bodies and the ministries or agencies responsible for formulating technical regulations.

Progress made in accreditation of laboratories, inspection bodies and certification bodies

For a number of products, importing countries do not consider manufacturers' declaration of conformity sufficient, and require imported products to be accompanied by a certificate of conformity assessment issued by a properly 'accredited' laboratory, inspection body or certification body. Though most of the case study countries appear to have laboratories, inspection bodies and certification bodies that carry out conformity assessment, an effective system for their accreditation by a recognized national accreditation body exists only in Malaysia. SIRIM QAS in Malaysia provides inspection services and audits on behalf of foreign certification bodies and purchasers. There are several arrangements at certification body and accreditation body level between organizations in Malaysia and those in other countries. If the situation in the other case studies is taken as illustrative of the situation in many developing countries, it would appear that most developing countries need assistance for establishing national accreditation bodies or for having conformity assessment bodies accredited by a foreign or regional accreditation body.[6]

Capacities for ensuring that imported goods conform to TBT regulations and SPS measures

All the case study countries appear to have established mechanisms to ensure that imported products meet the standards prescribed in their technical regulations and sanitary and phytosanitary measures. Their effectiveness in preventing imports of goods that do not meet prescribed standards or are sub-standard depends, however, on the efficiency with which the customs and other administrative departments apply border control measures, as well as the availability of laboratory facilities and trained personnel required for undertaking inspections and carrying out tests.

Technical assistance: identified needs and suggested delivery mechanism

Recommendations and observations in the joint report of the consultants

The consultants, who had worked separately on the preparation of the case studies, also submitted a joint report giving their views on the strengths and weaknesses of existing technical assistance programmes and on how all these programmes could be strengthened and oriented to make them more responsive

---

6   Currently there is no operational regional accreditation body.

to the needs of different developing countries, taking into account the stage reached by them in standardization development. Some of the observations made and views expressed by the consultants are listed below.

❑ Though considerable financial resources were being devoted by donor countries for providing assistance in the area of technical regulations and sanitary and phytosanitary measures, this amount fell far short of the total requirements for assistance by developing countries. In certain case study countries, there was a sense of frustration and a view was developing that their problems were not being taken seriously.

❑ Assistance required in the area of technical regulations and sanitary and phytosanitary measures was of a highly technical nature. The agencies in developed countries responsible for providing assistance on a bilateral basis did not always have the capacities needed to evaluate the proposals for assistance. The result was that in many cases the assistance provided did not reflect the needs and priorities of the recipient countries.

❑ In many cases, training was being provided on the application of technical regulations and the enforcement of sanitary and phytosanitary measures, without the countries being given the financial resources required to establish laboratory facilities and acquire equipment for testing. Alternatively, sophisticated laboratory equipment was provided even though the recipient country did not have the skilled human resources to make use of the facilities and operate the equipment. Technical assistance related to training had not always been effective.

❑ As many of the projects for capacity building did not insist on a contribution from the recipient countries, there was often no commitment on the part of the governments of the aid-receiving countries to support and continue the work after the initial infrastructure was established with aid money.

❑ There was a need for greater coordination among donor countries, and between donor countries and international organizations (both standard-setting and others), in providing technical assistance to developing countries.

❑ The need was emphasized to put greater reliance on South-South cooperation in providing assistance to improve the participation of developing countries in the work on formulating international standards, and in other trade-related standardization areas. In particular it was observed that 'it is vital for developing countries to learn from one another, rather than looking to developed countries for finding solutions to their problems'.

Specific areas for technical assistance

The specific areas in which technical assistance is needed include:

❑ Improving the participation of developing countries in standardization activities at international and regional levels, particularly in the work at technical level on formulation of draft standards for products of export interest to them;

❑ Creating greater awareness among industry and trade associations of the need to take a more active interest in standardization activities at both national and international level;

❑ Helping, on request, developing countries to meet the requirements of technical regulations and of sanitary and phytosanitary measures applicable in their export markets;

❑ Assisting interested developing countries to establish systems for alerting exporters to forthcoming changes in technical regulations or sanitary and phytosanitary measures; and

❑ Helping, on request, developing countries to establish bodies (at national or regional levels) for accreditation of conformity assessment bodies, or to access the services of foreign accreditation bodies.

In developing technical assistance programmes in each of the above areas, it is necessary to ensure that the assistance provided:

❑ Takes into account the fact that the technical assistance needs of developing countries vary considerably from country to country, according to the stage reached by them in the development of the standardization infrastructure. Consequently, the assistance provided has to be tailored according to the needs of individual countries.

❑ Is transparent and does not result in duplication of the assistance provided by donor countries under their bilateral assistance programmes or by international standard-setting organizations and other international organizations.

Assistance aimed at improving the participation of developing countries in standardization activities at international level

The analysis in the case studies has clearly brought out that the major problem encountered by developing countries, particularly those considered as less advanced (on the basis of the stage reached by them in the development of the standardization and conformity assessment infrastructure), is lack of human resources. Most of them do not have personnel available in the national standard-setting bodies, or in the ministries and government departments that are responsible for participation in international or regional standardization activities, with knowledge and expertise in the specific scientific fields related to the products for which standards are being formulated.

A number of mechanisms for improving the participation of developing countries in international standardization activities have been adopted by international standard-setting organizations themselves, such as:

❑ Financial assistance to attend meetings
   – Payment of special allowance by the organization
   – Sponsorship by developed countries;

❑ Submission of comments on draft standards by e-mail;

❑ Reform of voting procedures to include postal or electronic voting;

❑ More equitable sharing between developed and developing countries of the right to host secretariats of technical committees;

❑ Having developing countries act as co-host of secretariats of technical committees and as co-chairpersons.

❑ Holding workshops prior to the meetings of technical committees; and

❑ Mentoring and twinning arrangements.

It will be noticed that, even though all these mechanisms are steps in the right direction, they are mainly directed to facilitating attendance at meetings by covering travel costs or in overcoming the problems that developing countries face as a result of financial constraints in standardization activities. Their direct contribution to assisting developing countries in overcoming the basic problem they face because of the lack of technical expertise is at best marginal, except for the mechanism of holding workshops prior to meetings of technical committees and that of mentoring and twinning arrangements.

Workshops prior to meetings of technical committees

Holding workshops for three to four days for officials from developing countries, prior to the meetings of technical committees, helps in improving understanding by the participating officials of issues under discussion in the relevant technical committee. It also facilitates attendance at the meeting of the committee as travel costs for coming to the workshop are met from technical assistance funds. The responsibility for arranging workshops prior to the meetings of technical committees would rest with international standard-setting organizations responsible for the formulation of standards.

Mentoring and twinning arrangements

The term 'mentoring and twinning arrangement' is applied to an arrangement under which a country with the technical capacity to provide assistance in particular fields agrees to provide assistance to those countries that are in need of it. International organizations play the role of coordinator and catalyst by assisting countries in negotiating such arrangements on a bilateral or plurilateral basis, by bringing together those countries that can act as 'mentors' and provide advice and 'twinning' with them those countries that need assistance. The actual areas of assistance, and the terms and conditions on which it will be provided, are left to be negotiated on a bilateral basis or a plurilateral basis between the interested mentor country and the country or countries wishing to obtain assistance.

The main advantages of the arrangements are twofold. First, the assistance provided is, from the point of view of countries receiving it, needs-based. Second, countries have the opportunity to shop around and select the 'mentor country' that is best equipped to provide the type of assistance they need.

Need to establish a forum to encourage countries to enter into mentoring and twinning arrangements, where feasible, on a South-South basis

A forum for negotiating mentoring and twinning arrangements should be established for reasons described below:

❑ It would further highlight the need to take practical measures to ensure improved participation of developing countries in international standardization activities, in order to ensure that the standards adopted do not pose problems of compliance for them and that adoption by the trading partners of developing countries does not result in the creation of unnecessary barriers to trade.

❑ The framework established could be used for providing assistance on other trade-related aspects of standardization and conformity assessment work. The areas in which mentor countries could provide such assistance include:

   – Assistance in formulating technical regulations and sanitary and phytosanitary measures and enforcing them;

   – Assistance in establishing accreditation bodies responsible for accreditation of laboratories and other conformity assessment bodies;

   – Practical training of officials from twinning countries in the standardization area in which they need such assistance, by seconding them to work in the standardization institutions in the mentoring countries;

   – Making available to requesting countries the services of technical personnel with expertise in the scientific field of the standards under formulation; and

– Assistance in complying with technical regulations and sanitary and phytosanitary measures applied to imported products by the mentoring countries.

❑ National standards vary from country to country, in particular between developing and developed countries. This is mainly due to differences in climatic and environmental conditions but also because of differences in processes and production methods. If these differences are to be adequately reflected in the technical work at international level on standards formulation so that international standards adopted are not based on the standards applied only in developed countries, it is necessary to ensure that, wherever possible, the assistance provided under the mentoring and twinning arrangements is extended to requesting countries by developing countries with the necessary expertise and technical competence.

Main features of the framework to be established for facilitating mentoring and twinning arrangements

The effectiveness of the mechanism in meeting the technical assistance needs of developing countries would greatly depend on how far the framework established is conducive to and effective in facilitating bilateral or plurilateral negotiations among participating countries for mentoring and twinning arrangements. Some suggestions regarding the principles and guidelines on which the mechanism could be based are made below.

❑ The programme under the mechanism would be implemented on a pilot basis.

❑ The implementing agency would be responsible for:

– Providing facilities for exchange of information on trade-related aspects of standardization and for consultations on problems and issues of interest and concern to the participating countries through its networks;

– Assisting institutions or agencies from the participating countries, engaged in work at the national level in the subject area, in building up the information technology infrastructures needed for exchange of information through its networks; and

– Assisting and encouraging participating countries to enter into formal and informal mentoring and twinning arrangements on a bilateral or plurilateral basis.

Participation in the programme would be open initially to a limited number of interested countries. It is recognized that the programme would be viable only if a sufficient number of countries, with the technical capacities to act as mentors and willing to provide advice and assistance, agreed to join it. The programme would be implemented in two stages. In the first stage, emphasis would be placed on providing assistance to developing countries to improve their participation in the technical level discussions on the formulation of standards on a selected limited number of products identified as being of export interest to those developing countries and on which work on standardization is being undertaken, or is likely to be undertaken, in one of the seven international standard-setting organizations.

In the second stage, the programme would be broadened to include the possibility of extending, through mentoring and twinning arrangements, assistance to other priority areas identified by the case studies.

Creating greater awareness among industry and trade associations of the need for active interest in standardization activities at national and international level

The case studies highlighted a general lack of awareness on the part of trade and business associations as well as consumer associations in most developing countries. This often results in their not taking an active interest in undertaking the analytical work and background research that are necessary for advising the national standard-setting bodies, ministries or other agencies which are responsible for participating in international standardization activities.

A few developing countries with a well-developed standardization infrastructure have also now adopted effective mechanisms for soliciting the views of industry on draft international standards. Industry is responding by devoting resources for undertaking the analysis and research needed to ensure that national standards and production methods are taken into account in the approach adopted to the discussions at international level.

Information packages should be developed to explain the procedures adopted for formulation and development of international standards and how the support provided by industry and business associations, through analysis and research undertaken by them, could ensure that international standards remain responsive to their national requirements for quality and safety and ensure that adoption of these standards by trading partners does not constitute unnecessary barriers to trade. Workshops should be organized to provide guidance to participating countries on the appropriate mechanisms for consultations at national level between governments, on the one hand, and industry and business associations and consumer associations, on the other hand, on the trade-related standardization issues under discussion at national, regional and international levels.

Assistance to developing countries in meeting the requirements of technical regulations and of sanitary and phytosanitary measures applied in their export markets

Provision of practical assistance

The Agreements on TBT and SPS both call on member countries to provide technical assistance to developing countries. Proposals to make the obligation to provide such assistance more binding are under consideration in the WTO discussions and negotiations on strengthening the provisions relating to technical assistance in the WTO Agreements.

Preparation of brochures explaining technical regulations and sanitary and phytosanitary measures applicable to certain products

It may be desirable to produce brochures explaining in simple language the sanitary and phytosanitary measures applied in selected import markets for certain products such as fresh fruits and vegetables, fish and fish products, and meat and meat products. The case studies indicate that, in a large number of cases, the problems encountered by exporters in relation to these and other agricultural products arise from a lack of knowledge of the requirements which have to be fulfilled in order to ensure that the products will be permitted entry by the importing country. Exporters also face problems because requirements vary from one importing market to another.

Assistance to interested developing countries for establishing systems to alert exporters to changes in technical regulations or sanitary and phytosanitary measures

The Agreements on TBT and SPS impose obligations on countries adopting regulations or measures that deviate from international standards, to notify the products covered by them to the WTO Secretariat if they may have a significant effect on trade. Immediately on receipt these notifications are transmitted by the WTO Secretariat to the member countries for onward transmission to industry and business associations and are posted on the WTO website. The purpose of the notification procedure is to provide an opportunity for interested governments to comment on the draft regulations, so that the characteristics of products produced in their countries are adequately taken into account in adopting the final regulation.

The case studies have shown that many developing countries have not been able to make adequate use of this right to comment on draft regulations. This is because the government departments responsible for further processing such notifications simply do not circulate them to the industry and trade associations.

Notifications also serve to warn exporting countries that new regulations or measures are being adopted, or the existing ones are being modified. Exporters need help in preparing themselves to meet the requirements of new technical regulations or sanitary and phytosanitary measures in countries to which they export. There is a need for a 'model tool for alerting exporters' of the changes in requirements that are likely to occur as a result of the adoption of new technical regulations or sanitary and phytosanitary measures and conformity assessment systems.

Assistance for the establishment of accreditation bodies at national and regional level

The case studies have shown that national accreditation bodies do not exist in most of the countries or are not recognized at international level. In relation to imported products for which importing countries require conformity assessment there is reluctance to accept certificates issued by laboratories, inspection bodies or certification bodies that are not accredited. This often results in the imported products having to undergo further tests and inspections on importation.

A number of countries therefore need technical assistance to establish a government-recognized professional body to accredit laboratories and other conformity assessment bodies, after evaluation and site inspections undertaken in accordance with the guidelines adopted by the relevant international organizations. For some countries, it may be desirable and appropriate to establish such bodies at a regional level, or make arrangements for accreditation of conformity assessment bodies by a foreign accreditation body.

Concluding observations

Considerable emphasis has been placed on the mechanism of 'mentoring and twinning arrangements', particularly for providing assistance to improve the participation of developing countries in the work at technical level in international standardization activities.

The extent to which this mechanism would be effective in meeting the needs of developing countries for such technical assistance would depend in the main on two factors.

First is the existence of political will on the part of the governments of countries with the technical capacities to provide assistance directly to countries needing such assistance by entering into mentoring and twinning arrangements. In this context, it is important to keep in mind that in some of these countries national standard-setting and other bodies engaged in standardization work have a degree of autonomy.

The second related factor is the availability of financial resources to cover the cost of the technical assistance provided. Countries would be more willing to act as mentors if they were assured that adequate funds from multilateral institutions or from donor countries would be available over a reasonably long period of time to meet the costs and fees related to the provision of such assistance.

CHAPTER 1

Description of the main features and rules of the Agreements on TBT and SPS

General

The number of technical regulations is steadily on the increase in most countries. The trend is the response of regulatory authorities to growing public demand that products marketed should meet minimum quality and safety standards, and not have any adverse impact on the health and safety of the consuming public and on the environment. The same considerations often impel regulatory authorities to set and apply stricter sanitary and phytosanitary measures. Box 2 contains an illustrative

<table>
<tr><td colspan="2">Box 2
Illustrative list of import products subject to technical regulations and sanitary and phytosanitary measures</td></tr>
<tr><td colspan="2" align="center">Products subject to technical regulations</td></tr>
<tr><td>Machinery and equipment</td><td>Boilers
Electricity-driven construction and assembly tools
Metal and wood-working equipment
Medical equipment
Food-processing equipment</td></tr>
<tr><td>Consumer articles</td><td>Pharmaceuticals
Cosmetics
Synthetic detergents
Household electric appliances
Video and TV sets
Cinematographic and photographic equipment
Automobiles
Toys
Food (e.g. nutritional labelling)</td></tr>
<tr><td>Raw materials and agricultural inputs</td><td>Fertilizers
Insecticides
Hazardous chemicals</td></tr>
<tr><td colspan="2" align="center">Products subject to sanitary and phytosanitary measures</td></tr>
<tr><td>Fresh fruits and vegetables
Plants
Animals</td><td>Timber
Fruit juices and other food preparations
Meat and meat products</td></tr>
</table>

list of products for which countries apply mandatory quality and safety regulations and of agricultural products to which sanitary and phytosanitary measures are applicable in most countries.

Though such technical regulations and sanitary and phytosanitary measures are adopted by countries to attain legitimate policy objectives, they could in practice be used to provide disguised protection for domestic production.

International rules governing the application of mandatory technical regulations are contained in the Agreement on Technical Barriers to Trade (TBT). The Agreement on the Application of Sanitary and Phytosanitary Measures (SPS) lays down rules which countries must abide by in applying such measures. The basic aim of the detailed rules and guidelines in the two Agreements is to ensure that technical regulations and sanitary and phytosanitary measures are not formulated and applied by countries to create unnecessary obstacles to trade. The Agreements visualize that this could be attained if, wherever appropriate and possible, countries use international standards in formulating their technical regulations and sanitary and phytosanitary measures, and in developing national standards. Likewise, the Agreements call on them to use guidelines and recommendations developed by the international standard-setting bodies as a basis for their conformity assessment procedures.

As an incentive for countries to use international standards, the two Agreements provide that where international standards, guides or recommendations have been used as a basis for technical regulations, sanitary and phytosanitary measures, or conformity assessment procedures, it shall be presumed that they do not create unnecessary obstacles to trade. They further urge member countries to participate in the work of the international standard-setting bodies, so that international standards will be available for products for which they wish to adopt technical regulations or sanitary and phytosanitary measures, or develop voluntary standards. Countries are also urged to participate in the activities of such organizations in order to develop international guides and recommendations that can be used in developing national conformity assessment procedures.

Agreement on Technical Barriers to Trade

Definitions of the terms used: standards, technical regulations and conformity assessment procedures

International rules applicable to technical regulations for products used in trade in goods and the procedures used for assessment of conformity to such requirements are contained in the Agreement on Technical Barriers to Trade (TBT). The Agreement uses the term 'technical regulation' to cover norms with which compliance is mandatory. The term 'standard' is used to cover norms which are used on a voluntary basis.

Both terms cover:

❑ Product characteristics, including those relating to quality;

❑ Process and production methods that have an effect on product characteristics; and

❑ Conformity assessment procedures.

In the case of a large number of products entering international trade, buyers and regulatory authorities rely on the manufacturers' declaration of conformity with technical regulations or standards. In the case of some products, however, the authorities in importing countries require that domestically produced or imported products can be marketed only after they are certified by that country's regulatory authorities to conform to the technical regulations. The procedures adopted by regulatory authorities to certify that products conform to technical regulations are known as conformity assessment procedures. The latter also apply to certification on a voluntary basis to standards.

The Agreement defines a conformity assessment procedure as 'any procedure used, directly or indirectly, to determine that relevant requirements in technical regulations and standards are fulfilled'. In particular, the term includes:

❑ Testing and inspection;

❑ Certification of conformity of products;

❑ Certification of quality management systems; and

❑ Accreditation of bodies responsible for the above work.

Obligations to use international standards

The basic aim of the Agreement on TBT is to ensure that:

❑ Technical regulations and standards including packaging, marking and labelling requirements; and

❑ Procedures used for assessment of conformity with such technical regulations and standards

are based on international standards so as not to create unnecessary obstacles to trade.

However, there may be cases where internationally developed standards or guidelines are not available, or they may be considered by a country to be inappropriate or ineffective in achieving national objectives, perhaps for climatic and geographical reasons or for fundamental technological factors. Where the use of the international standard is considered to be inappropriate in developing a national technical regulation or standard, or where international standards do not exist, countries are free to develop their own national standards. Likewise, a country may adopt a conformity assessment system that is not based on the internationally accepted guidelines or recommendations if it considers that the technical content of the international guidelines is not suitable for the achievement of the specific objective of the proposed national system. However, in all such cases, where the proposed measures are expected to have a significant effect on trade, the Agreement imposes an obligation on the countries:

❑ To publish a notice about the proposed technical regulations, and conformity assessment procedures, and draft standards;

❑ To give reasonable opportunity to interested parties to comment on them; and

❑ To take into account these comments before finalizing the standards, technical regulations and conformity assessment procedures.

Further, in order to ensure that all countries interested in trade in products for which draft technical regulations and conformity assessment procedures have been formulated are able to comment on them, the countries formulating them are required to notify to the WTO Secretariat the products covered by the draft regulations, and their objectives and rationale. Such notifications are circulated by the WTO Secretariat immediately to member countries so that they can be brought to the attention of interested industries and other stakeholders.

Other specific rules

In order to ensure that technical regulations and voluntary standards do not create unnecessary barriers to trade, the Agreement on TBT further lays down certain principles and rules. It calls on regulatory agencies to ensure that technical regulations and standards:

❑ Are applied so as not to discriminate among imported products by the source of their origin (MFN principle);

❑ Do not extend to imported products treatment that is less favourable than that extended to domestically produced products (national treatment principle); and

❑ Are, where relevant, based on scientific and technical information; and

❑ Are not formulated or applied in a manner so as to cause 'unnecessary obstacles to trade'.

Agreement on the Application of Sanitary and Phytosanitary Measures

General

So far the discussion has centered on technical regulations, standards and systems for conformity assessment. The international rules applicable in these areas, which are contained in the Agreement on TBT, apply to both industrial and agricultural products. Imported agricultural products may, in many cases, have to conform not only to technical regulations but also to sanitary and phytosanitary measures that a country has adopted.

Definition of sanitary and phytosanitary measures

What are sanitary and phytosanitary measures? And how do they differ from technical regulations? For the purposes of the Agreement on SPS, sanitary and phytosanitary measures are defined as any measures applied:

❑ To protect human or animal life from risks arising from additives, contaminants, toxins or disease-causing organisms in their food;

❑ To protect human life from plant- or animal-carried diseases;

❑ To protect animal or plant life from pests, diseases, or disease-causing organisms;

❑ To prevent or limit other damage to a country from the entry, establishment or spread of pests.

The term 'sanitary measure' is used to cover regulations whose basic objective is to ensure food safety, or to prevent animal-borne pests or diseases entering the country. Where the objective of the measure is to ensure that imported plant varieties do not bring into the country plant-borne pests or diseases, it is called 'a phytosanitary measure'.

Control, inspection and approval procedures check and ensure the fulfilment of sanitary and phytosanitary measures. Those procedures include procedures for sampling, testing and certification.

The basic difference between technical regulations and sanitary and phytosanitary measures arises from the difference in objectives for which they are adopted. In the case of sanitary and phytosanitary measures, the aim is limited and specific – to protect human, animal and plant life and health by ensuring food safety and preventing animal and plant-borne pests or diseases entering the country. Technical regulations, on the other hand, are adopted for the attainment of a variety of policy objectives. They include national security requirements, prevention of deceptive practices and protection of the environment. They may also be adopted for the protection of human health or safety, or for the protection of animal or plant life, by means other than those covered by sanitary and phytosanitary measures (see box 3 for examples).

Box 3

Distinction between technical regulations and sanitary and phytosanitary measures: some examples

Whether a particular regulation adopted by a country for the protection of the life and health of its human and animal population or its plants is a technical regulation, or a sanitary or phytosanitary measure, depends on the objectives for which it has been adopted. The distinction is important, as the rules of the Agreement on TBT apply if the measure is treated as a technical regulation, and those of the Agreement on SPS if it is treated as a sanitary or phytosanitary measure. Although in most respects the provisions of the two Agreements are similar, there are some significant differences.

Broadly speaking, a measure would be considered as a sanitary and phytosanitary measure where the objective is to protect:

❑ *Human life from the risks arising from additives, toxins, or plant- and animal-carried diseases;*

❑ *Animal life from the risks arising from additives, toxins, pests, diseases, or disease-causing organisms;*

❑ *Plant life from the risks arising from pests, diseases, or disease-causing organisms; and*

❑ *A country from the risks arising from damage caused by the entry, establishment or spread of pests.*

Measures adopted for other purposes in order to protect human, animal and plant life would be treated as technical regulations.

The following examples would be helpful in understanding how the objective of the regulation determines whether it is a technical regulation, or a sanitary and phytosanitary measure (SPS). The examples demonstrate that the objective of a measure is decisive with regard to what Agreement it would fall under:

Regulation regarding pesticides

❑ *SPS if related to residues in food or in animal feed, and the objective is one of protecting human or animal health.*

❑ *TBT if related to the quality or efficacy of the pesticide, or health risk to handlers.*

Establishment of labelling requirements for foods

❑ *SPS if related to food safety.*

❑ *TBT if the regulation concerns issues such as type size, nutrient content, grade, etc.*

Regulation regarding containers for the shipment of grains

❑ *SPS if related to fumigation or other treatment of these containers, i.e. disinfection in order to prevent the spread of pests.*

❑ *TBT if related to the size or structure of the containers.*

Source: *WTO documents.*

Approach of the Agreement on SPS

The rules governing the use of sanitary and phytosanitary measures are contained in the Agreement on the Application of Sanitary and Phytosanitary Measures. The Agreement on SPS requires countries:

❑ To base their sanitary and phytosanitary measures on international standards, guidelines or recommendations developed by relevant international standard-setting bodies;

❑ To play a full part in the activities of the international organizations, in order to promote the harmonization of sanitary and phytosanitary measures on an international basis;

❑ To provide an opportunity to interested parties in other countries to comment on draft sanitary and phytosanitary measures when they are not based on international standards, when they deviate from them or when there are no international standards; and

❑ To accept the sanitary and phytosanitary measures of exporting countries as equivalent if they achieve the same level of sanitary and phytosanitary protection and, where possible, to enter into arrangements for mutual recognition of the equivalence of specified sanitary or phytosanitary measures.

Main differences between the two Agreements

The rules of the Agreement on SPS differ from those of the Agreement on TBT in four important respects.

First, there is a significant difference in the importance attached to 'scientific evidence' in formulating measures under the two Agreements. In the case of sanitary and phytosanitary measures, the obligation to base them on scientific evidence is unequivocal. The Agreement prescribes that such measures must be 'based on scientific principles and not maintained without any scientific evidence'. The Agreement on TBT, on the other hand, recognizes that the use of scientific evidence would depend on the objectives for which the technical regulations are adopted. Regulations adopted for the purposes of protecting health and safety would have to be based on scientific evidence; however, these considerations may not be relevant where the objective of the regulation is prevention of deceptive practices, or where it is adopted for national security reasons.

Second, the Agreement on TBT requires that technical regulations laying down product specifications should be applied on an MFN basis to imports from all sources. Sanitary and phytosanitary measures, particularly those which aim at preventing animal- or plant-borne diseases entering the country, may be more or less demanding depending on 'the level of prevalence of specific diseases or pests' in the country or in a region of that country. Imports may be allowed without any restrictions from countries that are free from certain types of diseases, while those from countries where such diseases are prevalent may be prohibited or subjected to quarantine or other regulations.

Against this background, the Agreement on SPS requires countries:

❑ To ensure that the measures taken are adapted to the sanitary and phytosanitary 'characteristics' of the area – whether all of a country or a part; such characteristics should be determined on the basis of the level of prevalence of pests or diseases; and

❑ Not to apply them so as to cause arbitrary or unjustifiable discrimination among countries or regions in countries where 'similar conditions' prevail, or constitute a disguised restriction on international trade.

It should be noted, however, that flexibility to deviate from the MFN principle is permitted only in the case of sanitary and phytosanitary measures that aim at preventing plant or animal pests and diseases from entering the country. Sanitary and phytosanitary measures aimed at ensuring food safety (e.g. regulations concerning use of additives, contaminants or permitted residue levels) would have, however, to be applied generally on an MFN basis.

Third, there are differences between the rules of the two Agreements regarding conditions under which it may be possible for countries to deviate from international standards. Many of these differences arise because of the differences in the objectives for which technical regulations and sanitary or phytosanitary measures are adopted. The Agreement on TBT, for instance, lays down specific conditions under which countries may deviate from international standards. The Agreement states that where an international standard exists, a country may adopt a national standard which is different or higher than the international standard if it is considered necessary, for 'fundamental climatic or geographical factors or fundamental technological problems'. The Agreement on SPS, on the other hand, gives the right to countries to introduce sanitary and phytosanitary measures that result in a 'higher level of protection' than would be achieved by measures based on relevant 'international guidelines or recommendations':

❑ If there is a scientific justification; or

❑ Where a country determines on the basis of assessment of risks that a higher level of sanitary and phytosanitary protection is appropriate.

In order to ensure that, in all cases where a country decides that higher standards than those laid down by international standards are appropriate, decisions are taken on an objective basis, the Agreement on SPS lays down certain guidelines that should be followed in assessing the risks to human, animal or plant life or health. These are listed in box 4.

In carrying out such risk assessment countries are urged to use risk assessment techniques developed by the relevant international organizations. In the dispute relating to the EU's ban on imports of hormone-treated meat brought to WTO, the Appellate Body observed that these provisions should not be interpreted to imply that a country that is planning to ban or restrict imports based on sanitary and phytosanitary measures must itself carry out the risk assessment. The country could rely on the risk assessment carried out by other countries or by international organizations.

Fourth, in cases where relevant scientific evidence is insufficient, provisional sanitary and phytosanitary measures may be applied on the basis of available pertinent information, including that from the relevant international organizations as well as from sanitary and phytosanitary measures applied by other WTO members. The Agreement on TBT does not contain any such provision.

Box 4

Guidelines for assessment of risk and determination of the appropriate level of sanitary and phytosanitary protection

Countries shall ensure that their sanitary or phytosanitary measures are based on an assessment, as appropriate to the circumstances, of the risks to human, animal or plant life or health, taking into account risk assessment techniques developed by the relevant international organization. In assessing such risks, the following elements should be taken into account:

❑ *Scientific evidence;*

❑ *Methods for production, processing (and control) used in the exporting country;*

❑ *Prevalence of specific diseases and the existence of pests or disease-free areas in the exporting country;*

❑ *Ecological and environmental conditions (both the exporting and importing country adopting the sanitary and phytosanitary measure); and*

❑ *Facilities for sanitary and quarantine and other treatment (in the country adopting the measures).*

Further, where sanitary and phytosanitary measures are intended to protect 'animal or plant life or health', the assessment of risks should be made taking into account the above elements and economic factors, such as:

❑ *The potential damage in terms of loss of production or sales in the event of entry and resulting spread of pests and diseases;*

❑ *The likely costs of controlling or eradicating the pests or diseases if they were to be spread; and*

❑ *The relative cost-effectiveness of alternative approaches to limiting risks.*

The Agreement emphasizes that, in adopting sanitary and phytosanitary measures, countries should keep in mind the need to ensure that the measures taken are not more trade-restrictive than required to achieve the appropriate level of protection, taking into account both technical and economic factors.

International standard-setting organizations: procedures and practices followed in formulating and adopting standards

General

The Agreements on TBT and SPS impose obligations on WTO member countries to use international standards as a basis for the technical regulations and the sanitary and phytosanitary measures that they apply. They also urge member countries to participate, to the fullest extent possible, in the activities of international standard-setting bodies, so that international standards for products and in areas where they wish to apply such regulations or measures are readily available.

There are around 50 organizations which are at present engaged in developing international standards. However, only a few of these organizations develop trade-related standards. The Agreement on SPS specifies that the obligation it imposes to apply international standards in order to ensure that the measures taken do not constitute unreasonable barriers to trade, applies to the standards developed, in particular, by the following three organizations:

❑ Codex Alimentarius Commission (CAC);
❑ Office International des Epizooties (OIE);
❑ International Plant Protection Convention (IPPC).

It is, however, open to member countries under the provisions of the Agreement to decide that standards developed by organizations other than these 'three sisters' should also be taken into account in formulating sanitary and phytosanitary measures.

The Agreement on TBT does not specify any international standardizing body; it is, however, generally recognized that its rules requiring countries to use international standards in formulating and adopting technical regulations apply to standards developed by:

❑ International Organization for Standardization (ISO);
❑ International Electrotechnical Commission (IEC);
❑ International Telecommunication Union (ITU);
❑ International Organization of Legal Metrology (OIML).

In this context it is relevant to note that the WTO Committee on TBT at its second triennial review in 2000 adopted a set of principles for international standards development including transparency, openness, impartiality and consensus, effectiveness and relevance, and coherence. This will help developing countries identifying international standards as a basis for their technical regulations.

Overview of the procedures and practices followed in adopting international standards

General

The seven organizations[7] mentioned above, which are engaged in developing trade-related international standards, vary considerably in their organizational forms and the systems adopted by them for their governance. The procedures that they follow in undertaking technical work for the development of standards also show considerable differences.

Box 5 summarizes, for each of these international standard-setting bodies:

❑ The main areas of standardization covered by its work;

❑ Its organizational form – whether non-governmental or intergovernmental; and

❑ Its membership and rights of members.

Organizational forms

Of the four international organizations that formulate standards used in technical regulations, two – ISO and IEC – are non-governmental (private sector) organizations. The bulk of the international standards for industrial products are formulated by these organizations. Of the remaining two, ITU is an intergovernmental organization belonging to the United Nations family. Although OIML is also an intergovernmental organization, it does not belong to the United Nations family.

All three organizations responsible for formulating standards that could be used in sanitary and phytosanitary measures are intergovernmental organizations. CAC is jointly managed by FAO and WHO; FAO also provides the secretariat for IPPC. OIE is an intergovernmental organization that does not belong to the United Nations family.

Pattern of membership

Who can become a member?

The pattern of membership also shows some variations. In the case of ISO, members are national standard-setting bodies. These are generally autonomous bodies engaged in formulation of standards at national level. Around two-thirds of these bodies belong to the public sector while the rest are private sector non-profit organizations. Members of IEC are 'national committees'; these are composed of, *inter alia*, manufacturers producing electrotechnical equipment and government agencies responsible for work in the area. The members of the remaining organizations (ITU, OIML, CAC, IPPC and OIE) are primarily governments. The ministries responsible for work at national level, in the areas of standardization covered by the concerned organizations, are primarily responsible for representing their countries in these organizations.

---

7   WHO has not been included because it is concerned, first and foremost, with safeguarding public health and not with trade.

Box 5
International standard-setting organizations

I. ORGANIZATION RESPONSIBLE FOR THE PREPARATION OF STANDARDS USED AS A BASIS FOR TECHNICAL REGULATIONS

ISO	IEC	ITU	OIML
A. Main areas of standardization			
All products and systems not falling within the competence of IEC and ITU.	Electrotechnical standards.	Telecommunications.	Legal metrology and measuring instruments.
B. Organizational form			
Non-governmental organization.	Non-governmental organization.	United Nations specialized agency.	Intergovernmental organization.
C. Membership and rights			
1. Who can become members			
National standards bodies.	National committees consisting, inter alia, of government agencies and manufacturers.	Governments and scientific or industrial associations.	Governments.
2. Classes of members and their rights			
93 member bodies, with the right to participate in all activities and to vote. 36 correspondent members who can attend as observers but have no right to participate in the work of technical committees and to vote. 14 subscriber members, who receive ISO bulletins and other publications.	52 full members with the right to participate actively and to vote. 11 associate members who can participate as observers but have no right to vote.	189 member governments. 670 sector members and associates. (Associates have limited rights of collaboration within the study groups and meetings. Sector members have access to various meetings and to publications, documents, information and statistics.)	58 member States, which participate actively in technical activities. 49 corresponding members, who attend as observers and have no right to vote.

II. ORGANIZATION RESPONSIBLE FOR FORMULATION OF STANDARDS USED AS A BASIS FOR SANITARY AND PHYTOSANITARY MEASURES

CAC	IPPC	OIE
A. Main areas of standardization		
Food quality and safety.	Phytosanitary measures and prevention of plant diseases.	Control of animal diseases. Trade in animals and animal products.
B. Organizational form		
Intergovernmental body jointly managed by FAO and WHO.	Multilateral treaty administered by FAO.	Intergovernmental organization but not member of the United Nations family.
C. Membership and rights		
1. Who can become members		
Governments (FAO and/or WHO members and/or associate members).	Governments (FAO members and non-members).	Governments.
2. Classes of members and their rights		
167 member governments. All members have the same status.	117 contracting parties to 1979 Convention. All members have the same status.	162 member governments. All members have the same rights, irrespective of the membership fees they pay.

Organizations having only one class of membership

In the intergovernmental organizations belonging to the United Nations family and engaged in standardization work – ITU, CAC, and IPPC – and in OIE, which does not belong to the United Nations family, members have the same status. All of them have a right to participate in all aspects of the ongoing work and have a right to vote. The other organizations have created different classes of membership, mainly with a view to facilitating participation of developing countries in their work.

Organizations having different classes of membership

ISO has, for instance, three classes of membership. Member bodies can participate in all activities of the organization and have the right to vote. Correspondent members can attend meetings as observers, but have no right to vote; these members are also not eligible to participate actively in the work of technical committees. In addition, there are subscriber members, who are entitled to get ISO bulletins and other publications but have no right to participate in the meetings of technical committees.

The IEC membership pattern closely follows that of ISO. It has full members, who can participate in all activities of its work and have the right to vote, and associate members, who can attend meetings as observers but have no right to vote and cannot actively participate in work of the technical committees. IEC has also recently adopted the 'Affiliate Country Programme' to create greater awareness of its work in developing countries that are not its members and to assist them in establishing 'national committees' that can participate in its work when they become members. Likewise, OIML has member States and corresponding members. Corresponding members can attend meetings only as observers and cannot vote.

Almost all members in the correspondent, associate or subscriber classes are developing countries. At ISO, 35 out of 37 correspondent members are from developing countries. These classes of membership have been established by the organizations to create awareness of the importance of their work among countries that are not in a position to become full members and to prepare them gradually for full membership by familiarizing them with their work. By creating these classes of membership, it has been also possible for the organizations to keep down the cost of membership: fees payable for these classes of membership are generally considerably lower than those payable for full membership.

Membership fees

Intergovernmental organizations belonging to the United Nations family

As box 6 shows, member countries do not pay separate fees for standardization work done by intergovernmental organizations belonging to the United Nations family. ITU meets the cost of standardization work from its budget; the expenses of CAC are met jointly by FAO and WHO; and the cost of the IPPC Secretariat is met from the budget of FAO.

Other intergovernmental and non-governmental organizations

Member countries have to pay separate fees for membership of intergovernmental organizations, such as OIML and OIE, and non-governmental organizations, such as ISO and IEC. However, all these organizations, except OIML, use criteria that result in developing countries paying fees that are lower than those charged to developed countries. Thus, in the case of ISO, contributions of each member country to its budget are determined by criteria that take into account such economic indicators as 'per

---

Box 6
Membership fees

A. INTERGOVERNMENTAL ORGANIZATIONS BELONGING TO THE UNITED NATIONS FAMILY

ITU	*The fee for member governments is proportional to the number of units from 1/8 to 40 that the States have freely chosen (one unit for the biennium 2002/03 is SwF 315,000). The 1/16 class is reserved for member governments from developing countries and other members as determined by the Council.*
	The minimum fee for sector members at the present time for ITU-T and ITU-R is ½ unit; for ITU-D it is 1/8 unit. Sector members from LDCs pay at least 1/16 unit (one unit for the biennium 2002/03 is SwF 63,000).
	The fee for associate members is based on the contribution unit for sector members as determined by Council for any particular biennial budgetary period. For the biennium 2002/03 the fee for associates participating in ITU-T is SwF 10,500, and for participating in ITU-D is SwF 3,937.50. Associate members from developing countries pay SwF 1,968.75.
CAC	*Member countries do not pay annual dues to the Commission. The expenditure of the Commission is met jointly by FAO (81 per cent) and WHO (19 per cent).*
	The members that host the specialist subordinate committees and task forces finance the secretariat work and provide a chairperson for the Committee.
IPPC	*FAO provides the secretariat for IPPC. The regular programme budget of the secretariat provides core resources for the work programme.*

B. OTHER INTERGOVERNMENTAL AND NON-GOVERNMENTAL ORGANIZATIONS

I. Intergovernmental organizations

OIML	*OIML's expenses are covered by annual contributions from member States. Countries are divided into four categories on the basis of their populations. Countries with small populations pay contributions that are lower than those payable with high populations. In 2002 the annual membership fee for countries in the first category was 12,002 euros; for those in the fourth category it was 48,004 euros. The annual membership fee for corresponding members was 914 euros in 2002.*
OIE	*Members of OIE pay an annual fee. The countries are divided into six categories. In 2001 fees ranged from 12,264 euros to 102,175 euros. Members are free to choose the category to which they wish to be assigned.*

II. Non-governmental organizations

ISO	*Two-thirds of the expenses of the central secretariat are met by contributions from its members. The balance is met by revenues derived from sale of standards, copyright royalties, etc.*
	The contribution of each member is determined by a formula that takes into account such economic indicators as per capita GNP, value of exports and imports, and involvement in standardization and is fixed by a number of units based on these factors.
	The value of one unit was fixed at SwF 5,661 for 2002.
	• *Member bodies pay fees ranging from 5 to 170 units (SwF 28,305 to SwF 1,528,470);*
	• *Correspondent members pay 2 to 4 units (SwF 11,322 to SwF 22,644); and*
	• *Subscriber members pay ½ unit (SwF 2,830).*
	The costs associated with working within TCs/SCs are borne directly by the participants, and the member bodies holding the secretariat of those committees directly finance the secretariat work.
IEC	*About 60 per cent of the expenditures of the central secretariat are met by contributions from member countries; the remainder is financed by the sale of publications and other sources approved by the Council.*
	The contribution of each member is determined taking into account such criteria as GNP and annual electricity consumption per capita, provided that these are equal to or higher than the minimum percentage agreed by Council as qualifying for full membership.
	Associate members pay annual dues equivalent to half their calculated percentage of dues.
	The member providing host facilities finances the secretariat at work.

capita GNP, value of exports and imports, and involvement in standardization activities'. In the case of IEC the criterion is based on GNP and annual electricity consumption per capita. OIE has divided its fee structure into six categories; countries are free to choose the category to which they wish to be assigned. The criterion used by OIML is the size of population; countries with a small population (less than 10 million) pay one-quarter of the contribution made by those with a big population (more than 100 million).

The fees charged by international standard-setting bodies with different classes of membership are generally lower for correspondent or associate membership than for full membership.

The subscriber members of ISO pay only a small token fee, as do correspondent members of OIML. Countries do not pay any fees to participate in the Affiliate Country Programme of IEC.

It is important to note that the fees paid by member countries go to finance the expenditure of the secretariats of these organizations. In the case of organizations such as ISO, IEC and CAC, where technical work on the formulation and development of standards is undertaken in technical committees or committees hosted by one of the member countries, the entire cost of providing technical support and secretariat facilities is met by the country providing the support.

Procedures for the formulation of standards

Procedures adopted for technical work on formulation of standards

The procedures adopted by international standard-setting organizations for work at technical level on the formulation of standards show marked variations. Each organization's procedure is greatly influenced by the practices followed by it in the past and by the framework adopted by it for decision-making on administrative and technical matters. In the case of international standard-setting bodies belonging to the United Nations family, the procedures used for work in the standardization field are also influenced by the practices they follow for work in other areas.

Even though procedures adopted by different international organizations vary widely at the detail level, there are a few principles and elements that are common to all of them. These are described below.

❑ The decision to commence work for a new standard is taken by the relevant body within the organization that is responsible for making such decisions, at the request of a member or a group of members or on an initiative taken by the secretariat.

❑ Once the decision is taken and the definition and technical scope of the standard are agreed upon, the responsibility for 'negotiating technical specifications' and 'for consensus building' on the draft standard is assigned:

– In the case of ISO, IEC and OIML, to technical committees and sub-committees;

– In the case of ITU, to study groups;

– In the case of CAC, to general subject or commodity committees or to ad hoc intergovernmental task forces;

– In the case of OIE, to one of the specialist commissions; and

– In the case of IPPC, to working groups.

❑ The draft standard prepared in discussions and negotiations at expert level is circulated by the secretariat to all members for comments and views.

❏ The comments received from members are passed on to the relevant committees or commissions for review and examination.

❏ The final draft is prepared by the committees or commissions, after taking into account the comments received from members. It is then transmitted to the apex body of the organization (CAC, OIE, IPPC) or the relevant committee (OIML) or full members (ISO, IEC) for adoption as an international standard.

It is important to note that there are, however, considerable differences among the seven organizations in the way in which the technical work on the formulation of standards is undertaken by the technical committees and commissions.

In the case of ISO and IEC, once the decision to assign the work to a technical committee is taken, the major responsibility for providing chairmanship, secretarial and technical support devolves on the member country that agrees to provide host facilities for undertaking the work. In CAC the work is given to a general subject or commodity committee or to an ad hoc intergovernmental task force hosted by a member country. The country providing host facilities also agrees to meet all expenditure relating to such work. The adoption of this decentralized system has been necessitated by both the volume of their work and the constraints put on them by the availability of financial resources. These three organizations (ISO, IEC, CAC) are responsible for organizing technical work for over 85 per cent of the trade-related standards developed every year. The standards adopted by them also cover a wide range of different products and subject areas. It would have been almost impossible for the personnel in the secretariats of these organizations to guide and supervise technical work in all these areas. Nor would they have been able to meet the cost of such technical work from their limited financial resources.

By making host countries responsible for coordinating technical and research work relating to the preparation of draft standards and for meeting the costs of the work, these organizations are able to meet the increasing demands that are being made on them. On the other hand, secretariats of other organizations such as IPPC, ITU and OIE, whose mandate covers only a limited range of product areas, are able to produce best results by arranging expert level meetings directly under the umbrella of their secretariats, and meet the costs of such work from their own budgets.

The decentralized system adopted by ISO, IEC and CAC does suffer from some limitations. The host country is best placed to show leadership in a specialist committee, and this gives it both prestige and influence.

Most developing countries do not possess the scientific personnel required for providing secretariat assistance and for supporting research facilities. A few developing countries that do have the expert human resources required are not able to make a bid to become hosts, as they lack the financial resources needed. The result is that in 2001, developed countries held over 90 per cent of the technical committees and sub-committees established by ISO and IEC. In the case of CAC, developed countries hosted 20 of the 23 committees.

Various proposals that would make it easier for developing countries to provide host facilities to technical committees are under consideration in these three organizations. In CAC, for instance, a proposal has been made that its permanent commodity or general subject committees should be replaced with time-limited ad hoc committees. Such a change would, it is expected, lead to greater rotation of secretariats among members, giving a chance to interested developing countries to make a bid for hosting the committees. Another proposal under consideration is that CAC members that hold secretariats of its commodity and general subject committees should involve developing country members as co-hosts and co-chairpersons. This is intended as an interim measure to provide developing countries with the experience of hosting CAC committees. At ISO proposals have been made to encourage committees to hold meetings in developing countries, to take major decisions by correspondence rather than at meetings, and to hold meetings only when absolutely necessary. In addition, while encouraging all member bodies to consider 'twinning' arrangements at all levels, member bodies in developing countries are encouraged to offer to host ISO meetings and apply for vacant committee secretariats. Participants in the IEC Affiliate Country Programme learn how to monitor relevant technical work in the technical committees with a view to establishing an IEC national committee and seeking IEC membership in the future.

Procedures for the adoption of international standards

The procedures adopted for taking decisions on the adoption of international standards on the basis of the draft standards developed in the work at technical level also differs among the international standard-setting bodies. As a principle, the procedures provide for adoption by consensus.

At CAC, for instance, if efforts to develop consensus fail, decisions are taken through voting and draft standards are adopted if a majority of the members vote in favour (in practice, however, this happens only on very rare occasions). The same procedure is followed by the International Committee of OIE. At IPPC draft standards are approved as international standards if majority vote is in favour.

In ISO and IEC as a rule, draft standards are not transmitted for adoption to the full members unless there is consensus among the countries participating in the work at technical level. Even after such consensus a formal vote is required for the draft standards to be adopted as international standards. The adoption criteria require approval by two-thirds of the ISO members that have participated actively in the standard development process and approval by 75 per cent of the members that vote. In the case of OIML a majority of two-thirds among participating members of technical committees is required for draft standards to be adopted as international standards.

Other measures taken by the international standard-setting bodies to facilitate participation of developing countries

In addition to adopting systems for determining annual contributions that result in lower levels of payments by developing countries, at present all of these organizations employ a variety of mechanisms that aim at facilitating participation of developing countries in their work. These include:

❑ Providing financial assistance to attend meetings;
❑ Allowing submission of written comments on proposals, and electronic voting;
❑ Establishing special committees for developing countries; and
❑ Holding workshops to improve participation of developing countries.

These measures taken by the international standard-setting organizations are complemented by the establishment of trust funds by international organizations such as WHO, FAO, WTO and the World Bank for, *inter alia*, facilitating attendance of developing countries at meetings and enhancing their capacities for participation in standardization activities. The main features of the actions taken by the international standard-setting organizations and by other international organizations are briefly discussed below.

Financial assistance to attend meetings

Payment of a special allowance by the organization

OIE pays a 'special allowance' to each member country with voting rights to attend the annual meetings of its International Committee. This has greatly improved attendance by developing countries, as it enables them to meet the costs of travel and accommodation during the period of the meeting.

Sponsorship by developed countries

Proposals that developed countries should agree to finance travel and other related expenditure of delegations from developing countries to attend technical level and other meetings, under their bilateral assistance programmes, are also under consideration in CAC and in IPPC. One potential problem of such assistance is that donor countries might sponsor travel and provide funding for other expenditure in order to gain the recipient country's support to the changes and modifications that they have suggested to the draft standards in the work at expert level. There are serious doubts as to whether these proposals will receive favourable consideration from donor countries, as the amounts required are expected to be large.

Holding workshops prior to technical committee meetings

CAC is using an innovative method to facilitate participation of developing countries in the technical level discussions in the commodity and general committees. It organizes workshops under technical assistance programmes on the subjects discussed in the committees a few days before their meetings. Participants in the workshops can then stay on for the meeting of the committee and take active interest in its work.

Sponsorship under ISO's Development Programme

Officers from developing countries and from countries in transition are sponsored to attend ISO technical committees that are of interest to them. A large number of developing countries have been sponsored to attend meetings of ISO/TC 176, *Quality management and quality assurance* and of ISO/TC 207, *Environmental management*.

Submission of comments on draft standards by e-mail

ISO accepts written comments on draft standards and there is evidence that developing countries take advantage of this to provide an input to the standard-setting process. Voting is undertaken by e-mail; ISO provides training in electronic balloting upon request to developing countries to ensure that they use their right to vote. At IEC the distribution of documents for standards production is 100 per cent electronic.

Establishment of special committees or projects

All seven organizations provide opportunities for discussions at the meetings of their apex bodies on how the capacities of developing countries for participation in their activities could be improved. They have also adopted programmes for holding workshops and training programmes for officials from these countries on topics covered by their work and for transfer of technology.

Furthermore, ISO and OIML have established special committees to discuss problems and issues of interest and concern to developing countries. The aim of the ISO Committee on Developing Country Matters (DEVCO), which meets once a year prior to its General Assembly meeting, is to identify the needs and requirements of developing countries in the fields of standardization and to assist them in meeting those needs. DEVCO has a three-year activity plan known as DEVPRO, which offers activities such as training, sponsorship and publications to its members. Likewise the Development Council of OIML provides a forum for discussions on activities of particular concern to developing countries and on how the assistance they need could be provided.

ITU has a project called Electronic Commerce for Developing Countries that aims to promote and coordinate programmes to accelerate technology transfer to developing countries. It also tries to stimulate cooperation between the public and private sectors to create technologies suited to developing countries.

The IEC Affiliate Country Programme offers to newly industrializing countries a form of participation in IEC. Participants have full use of IT tools to reduce costs of participation to virtually zero. The programme aims to encourage greater awareness and use of IEC International Standards and helps newly industrializing countries to understand and participate in the work of IEC.

Workshops for improving participation of developing countries

In 2000 the WTO Committee on TBT arranged a workshop for exchange of information and ideas on the problems faced by developing countries in respect of the implementation and operation of the Agreement on TBT. The recommendations adopted at the workshop envisage 'adoption of programmes by developed countries for providing technical assistance to improve expertise in developing countries through arranging training programmes and seminars and to making available to them experts', 'South-South cooperation by sharing information' and 'encouragement of mentoring and twinning arrangements among international standard-setting bodies'. For details see box 7.

Box 7

Workshop on technical assistance and special and differential treatment in the context of the Agreement on TBT, held by the Committee on TBT in Geneva, July 2000

During the workshop, problems and needs in four areas were identified: i) implementation and administration of the Agreement; ii) international standards; iii) conformity assessment procedures; and iv) capacity building. This box focuses on international standards.

Identified problems faced by developing country members

❑ *Lack of effective participation in international standard-setting bodies;*

❑ *Lack of expertise in the international standardization process;*

❑ *Operational constraints, such as the lack of human and financial resources;*

❑ *Absence of a clear definition of an international standard;*

❑ *Lack of translation of international standards into languages other than English and French;*

❑ *Relevancy of international standards to the needs of developing countries.*

Suggested solutions

❑ *Concerning the problem of participation:*

  • *Rotation of the secretariats or chairmanship of technical committees;*
  • *Use of e-mail and video conferencing as alternatives to traditional meetings;*
  • *Regional cooperation (South-South cooperation).*

➡

❑ *Concerning the level of expertise:*

- *Provision of technical assistance and training, e.g. through twinning;*
- *Mentorship agreements;*
- *Coordination and cooperation among international standard-setting bodies and WTO.*

❑ *Operational:*

- *Official translation of final version of international standards;*
- *Prioritizing international standardization activities related to products or subject-matter of particular interest to developing countries;*
- *Coordination at the national level.*

In September 2002 ISO arranged a workshop on 'Participation of Developing Countries in International Standardization'. The General Assembly, which considered the recommendations made by the workshop, has requested the ISO Council: 'to accelerate the implementation of the concept of the twinning arrangements as a means of building capacity ...; the use of ICT [electronic communication] to facilitate participation through electronic means; the implementation of the training programme, in particular through use of Internet, to increase participation of developing countries in international standardization.' For details see box 8.

Box 8

ISO General Assembly Workshop on 'Participation of Developing Countries in International Standardization' in Stockholm, September 2002

The workshop brought together the conclusions of five separate workshops held in different regions of the world (Belgrade, Bangkok, Nairobi, Bogotá, Cairo) in 2001 and 2002. Some of the main problems identified were:

❑ ***Lack of awareness***. *A firm or a government convinced that it would find benefit in participating in standards development work would be ready to contribute. However, to be convinced, stakeholder awareness is necessary.*

❑ ***Language***. *Information flows could dry up rapidly because of lack of people with the necessary knowledge of English to handle the information dispensed, as well as for technical work.*

❑ ***Locating experts***. *Lack of expertise to participate in technical meetings has been identified as a high problem area.*

A number of recommendations were made. Some of them are highlighted below.

National Standards Bodies (NSBs) should

❑ *Raise awareness of the role of standards for economic development in their countries;*

❑ *Identify, jointly with industry and government, areas of interest to the country in relation to the ISO technical programme;*

❑ *Cooperate and share resources when the full standardization, quality, testing and certification infrastructure is not concentrated in the NSB.*

Governments in developing countries should

❑ *Use standards as the basis for regulations.*   ➡

➡

The private sector should

❑ *Build capacity in metrology, standards, accreditation and certification as required.*

Donors should

❑ *Assist in developing capacity for the standardization infrastructure.*

International Organizations, including ISO, should

Help to enhance participation of developing countries in their work by:

❑ *Supporting secretariat rotation and twinning;*

❑ *Supporting greater involvement and commitment of developing countries in policy and TC/SC committee leadership levels;*

❑ *Providing incentives for active participation of developing countries;*

❑ *Developing guidelines and rules for stakeholder involvement in standards development.*

In 2002 WTO arranged a workshop on technical assistance and capacity building related to the Agreement on SPS. One conclusion emerging from the workshop was that the review and updating of the legal framework for sanitary and phytosanitary measures at the national level was an extremely important obstacle to implementing sanitary and phytosanitary measures in developing countries For details see box 9.

Box 9

Workshop on technical assistance and capacity building related to the Agreement on SPS, held by the Committee on SPS in Geneva, November 2002

Key messages emerging from the workshop included:

❑ *Importance of a needs-focused approach;*

❑ *Differences between countries and regions regarding technical assistance needs;*

❑ *Need to avoid duplication of effort;*

❑ *Need to improve coordination and cooperation among donor agencies; and*

❑ *Need for a holistic approach to technical assistance and capacity building.*

One conclusion was that the review and updating of the legal framework for sanitary and phytosanitary measures at the national level was an extremely important obstacle to implementing sanitary and phytosanitary measures in developing countries.

Actions by international organizations for facilitating participation of developing countries through establishment of trust funds

Boxes 10 and 11 describe the actions that have been taken recently by international organizations such as WHO, FAO, WTO, OIE and the World Bank to establish trust funds for, *inter alia*:

❑ Facilitating attendance of developing countries at meetings of organizations responsible for formulation of standards used in sanitary and phytosanitary measures;

❑ Improving their technical capacities for participation; and

❑ Helping them to develop capacities to implement international standards on food safety and on plant and animal health.

Box 10

FAO/WHO Trust Fund

The Codex Executive Committee approved a proposal for the creation of a 12-year trust fund to enhance the participation in CAC work of relevant experts from developing countries and countries in transition and to build national capacity. The trust fund, which is located in WHO and financed through voluntary contributions, was launched on 14 February 2003. The focal point for the project is Codex; its first priority is to facilitate attendance at meetings. Other aims of the project are:

❑ *To strengthen the capacity of countries to build strong and compatible food control systems;*

❑ *To ensure that experts in all countries understand the goals and objectives of Codex; and*

❑ *To provide pilot funding to enable a number of countries to develop effective proposals and information for Codex consideration.*

Box 11

Standards and Trade Development Facility (STDF)

In 2002 WTO, the World Bank, FAO, WHO and OIE launched an inter-agency global facility/framework for capacity building in sanitary and phytosanitary measures, with an initial amount of money from the World Bank and administered by WTO. The facility will assist developing countries in the development or improvement of national food safety, animal and plant health systems. The initiative includes four main components:

❑ *Enhancing scientific and technical expertise;*

❑ *Enhancing participation in the work of international standard-setting bodies;*

❑ *Developing tools; and*

❑ *Developing an information system.*

Level of participation of developing countries in international standardization activities: findings and conclusions of the case studies

General

From the description of the procedures in the previous chapter, it is clear that conscious efforts are being made by international organizations to facilitate the participation of developing countries in all aspects of their work. The question that arises is how far the measures taken have in practice resulted in greater and improved participation of developing countries as a group. One of the major aims of the case studies was to examine this question in the light of the practical experience of the participation of selected countries in international standardization activities, in order to gain greater insight into the technical assistance that is needed to ensure continued and effective participation of these countries in these activities. It is to the description of the findings and conclusions of the case studies on this aspect that this chapter is devoted.

It was recognized that the capacity of countries to participate in international standardization activities is greatly influenced by the progress made at national level in developing the infrastructure and institutional framework that are necessary for the development of activities relating to standardization and conformity assessment. Taking this into account, countries at differing levels of development were selected for the case studies. Malaysia was selected to represent countries, where 'institutions engaged in standardization and conformity assessment activities are relatively well developed'. Jamaica, Kenya, Mauritius and Uganda were chosen because 'some progress has been made' in establishing the framework. Namibia was selected as representing countries where 'work on standardization and conformity assessment is at a nascent stage'. These are generally the least developed countries (LDCs); some of them are also small economies.

Findings on the level of participation in the activities of the international standard-setting bodies

International standard-setting bodies producing standards used in sanitary and phytosanitary measures

Malaysia has achieved a high level of participation in the activities of all three organizations – CAC, IPPC and OIE – which develop standards that are used in sanitary and phytosanitary measures. It has not only been able to attend and participate in all meetings of the apex bodies of these organizations, but has also taken an active interest in participating in technical work on the development of a number of standards that are considered to be of national interest.

For example, it has participated in the work on developing CAC general guidelines on use of the term 'halal' for meat. It is actively participating in work of the Codex Committee on milk and milk products, in order to ensure that the international standards adopted for 'milk substitutes', which it produces from palm oil fats, are close to the national standards it has developed. Malaysia is also trying to play an active role in the drafting committees established under IPPC, for instance by participating actively in the drafting committee on timber products, in order to ensure that the standards adopted are not based entirely on the production processes and methods used by temperate timber producers but also take into account the needs of tropical timber producers.

Although Mauritius appears to have built up the administrative infrastructure required for participation in standardization activities, it has been able to take a very limited role in the actual work of international standard-setting bodies producing standards that are used in sanitary and phytosanitary measures. The only international standardization body whose meetings it has been attending on a regular basis is OIE, which covers part of the costs of participating delegations. It has not attended the annual meetings of IPPC, preferring to use its limited resources to attend some meetings of the WTO Committee on SPS. Mauritius has occasionally attended meetings of the Codex Committee on Sugars, but has not been able to take an interest in and attend meetings of its other technical committees. Apart from financial constraints, the limited interest it has been taking in the discussions on standardization issues in the area of SPS may be the result of the generally declining share of agricultural products in its total exports.

Jamaica has been able to attend some meetings of the apex body of CAC but not those of OIE and IPPC. Its attendance in meetings where technical work on standards formulation is undertaken is extremely limited and sporadic; it has participated in only two meetings of some Codex Committees.

Kenya has been able to participate actively in the meetings of the apex bodies of CAC, OIE and IPPC. However, it has not been able to participate in the technical work on the development of standards in any of these organizations, even though work that is being done in areas such as pesticide residues, food additives, fresh fruits and vegetables, milk and milk products is of interest for producers in the country.

Uganda participates in the meetings of the apex bodies of CAC and OIE. It is not a signatory to IPPC. It has attended four or so other meetings of CAC, although resources generally preclude attendance at technical committee meetings.

The case study for Namibia shows that it is able to attend only the meetings of the apex body of OIE. It has not participated in the technical work on the preparation of standards, as it does not have personnel with the necessary scientific background. Namibia attends OIE annual meetings, possibly because travel and other costs are made available by the organization. Namibia is not yet a signatory to IPPC and has not participated in meetings of CAC.

International standard-setting bodies producing standards used in technical regulations

As in the case of its participation in the activities of international standard-setting bodies formulating standards that are used in sanitary and phytosanitary measures, Malaysia has been able to achieve a reasonably high level of participation in the work of the organizations that are responsible for the formulation of standards used in technical regulations. Thus Malaysia participates in policy level discussions in the annual and other meetings of the apex bodies of ISO, IEC, and ITU. It also participates actively in the technical level discussions on standards formulation in sectors of export interest to its economy and is making constant efforts to broaden the scope of its participation in the technical committees, sub-committees and working groups in order to ensure that no sector which is of interest to the national economy is left without participation. Thus, the Department of Standards Malaysia, its national standard-setting body, together with SIRIM Berhad, participates in the annual General Assembly of ISO and in the meetings of CASCO and DEVCO. It is a participating member of 66 TCs/SCs and is an observer member of 124 TCs/SCs within ISO and IEC. In order to ensure that the interest and concerns of all interested stakeholders are fully reflected in the preparatory work in the TCs and SCs, proposed draft international standards are circulated for comments to the associations of industries, consumer associations, and other private sector organizations, and to public sector departments and their views are taken into account in formulating national positions on the development of international standards. The Department of Standards Malaysia provides the secretariat for ISO/TC 45, *Rubber and rubber products*; ISO/TC 45/SC 4, *Products other than hoses*; two working groups; and ISO/TC 157, *Mechanical contraceptives*. Lack of funds, however, prevents the country from participating on a regular basis in work at the technical level of all the committees of which it is a member or in which it has interest, and the country has to decide on priorities for participation.

Mauritius is a member of ISO and ITU. It is not a member of IEC but it regularly receives its standards under its 'registered subscription scheme' and participates in its Affiliate Country Programme. It is a corresponding member of OIML. It attends the ISO General Assembly and ISO DEVCO meetings, and attended meetings of ISO CASCO in the past. It has become a participating member in five ISO TCs including ISO/TC 176, *Quality management and quality assurance* and ISO/TC 207, *Environmental management*, and participates actively in their work. It hosted a meeting – TC 34/SC7, *Spices and condiments* – in 1997.

Jamaica is a member of ISO and ITU. It is not a member of IEC and OIML. However, it participates in the Affiliate Country Programme of IEC. It attends the annual ISO General Assembly and is at present on the ISO Council and was recently appointed to the ISO Developing Countries Task Force. It also attends meetings of ISO DEVCO and ISO CASCO. As regards participation in the work at technical level on standards formulation, even though it is a participating member of 20 ISO TCs/SCs and has observer status in 76 ISO TCs/SCs, it has been able to attend only one TC meeting, and that only because funds were made available under the ISO Development Programme. In recent years, it has been taking active steps to increase the involvement of industries and the business community in standardization activities. It has recently been decided that the decision on what standards should be developed should be led by industry. These measures are expected to influence positively the ability of the country to participate in international standardization activities.

Kenya is a member of ISO, ITU and OIML. It is not a member of IEC but participates in its Affiliate Country Programme. The Kenya Bureau of Standards is a member of the ISO Council and provides the ISO Regional Liaison Officer for Africa (excluding the Arab countries). Even though the Kenya Bureau of Standards is able to participate in the annual General Assembly of ISO, and its DEVCO and CASCO meetings, shortage of funds has prevented it from taking an active role in the work of technical committees.

The Uganda National Bureau of Standards, Uganda's national standard-setting body, is a correspondent member of ISO and participates in the Affiliate Country Programme of IEC. Uganda is not a member of OIML or ITU. The

Uganda National Bureau of Standards attends the annual General Assembly of ISO and its DEVCO meetings. There is no participation at the technical level in any international organization because of lack of technical expertise and financial resources.

The national standard-setting body of Namibia, the Namibian Standards Information and Quality Office, is a correspondent member of ISO and a participant in the Affiliate Country Programme of IEC. Namibia is a member of ITU but neither of OIML nor of IEC. The Namibian Standards Information and Quality Office attends the annual General Assembly of ISO. As a correspondent member, it is not able to participate actively in the technical work in ISO.

Lessons that can be drawn

Several lessons can be drawn from the analysis of the experience of the countries in the case studies.

First, countries like Malaysia are able today to participate in the work at all levels in the international standardization organizations in which they have an interest, taking into account the composition of their exports and imports. However, they cannot participate in all the working groups or technical committees in which they have an interest. The participation of most of the countries in the case studies is confined to attending the meetings of the apex bodies of these organizations. In most cases they are not able to attend the meetings of the working groups or technical committees, where work is undertaken at technical level on the formulation of standards for products of trade interest to them, because of financial and other constraints.

Second, most of the countries in the case studies do not appear to have at present the expertise needed for participation in the work at technical level on the formulation of standards. Even Malaysia, which has been participating actively in the technical work on formulating standards for products in which it has trade interest, has not been able to participate in the Codex Committee on Veterinary Drugs, because 'of lack of expertise in setting MRLs and assessing the value of different levels in terms of risk to human health'.

Thirdly, participation in standardization activities, particularly at technical level, is greatly facilitated if industry and interested business firms assist the agencies responsible for participating in the technical work, by carrying out background research and analytical work. In most developed countries, the main responsibility for undertaking such research and for writing of draft standards is taken by the interested industry. Industry also bears the cost of research. This also appears to be the situation in case of countries like Malaysia.

For most of the case study countries, one of the important tasks to be addressed is that of creating greater awareness among industry and trade groups of the need on their part to carry out the basic research and analytical work that is necessary for participation in the technical work on standardization at international level.

These considerations show that action taken by the international standard-setting bodies with a view to facilitating the participation of developing countries in their work would have to be complemented by action at national level. Further, it would be unrealistic to expect all developing countries to be able to participate in the technical work on formulation of standards for products of interest to them, even if the travel and other costs of officials are met by the international standard-setting organization itself or through the establishment of trust funds. Almost all countries in the study do not at present have the capacities to influence the outcome of discussions at technical level in these bodies because they do not, in most cases, have capacities to develop the analytical research data required for supporting their points of view.

CHAPTER 4

Participation of developing countries in regional standardization activities

General

The previous chapter described the findings of the case studies on the problems and difficulties faced by developing countries wanting to participate in international standardization activities. This chapter provides an overview of the findings of the case studies on work that is being done at regional level by these countries in the field of standardization.

The increasing emphasis which developing countries are giving to regional trade and economic cooperation has also resulted in greater attention being paid to work on standardization on a regional basis. This work in the standardization field constitutes an integral part of the measures taken by them for the promotion of intraregional trade.

Aims and objectives of standardization activities undertaken on a regional basis

Box 12 lists some of the regional standard-setting organizations in the activities of which the case study countries are participating.

Though there are some differences of emphasis and nuance, the broad aims and objectives of the activities undertaken on a regional basis in the standardization field are:

❑ Aligning domestic standards of member countries with international standards;

❑ Developing regional standards for products of importance in trade among member countries for which international standards have not been developed or are not likely to be developed;

❑ Enhancing the technical infrastructure and competence in testing, calibration, certification and accreditation based on internationally accepted procedures;

❑ Providing a mechanism for cooperation in accreditation at the regional level, and encouraging mutual recognition by countries in the region of one another's accreditation and conformity assessment systems; and

❑ Providing assistance for the development of the standards and conformity assessment infrastructure in countries in the region needing such assistance.

Box 12
Regional standard-setting organizations

AFRICA

❑ **African Regional Organization for Standardization (ARSO)**. *ARSO has developed a comprehensive programme on standardization and related activities for its member States. Its objectives are to promote standardization activities in Africa; elaborate and harmonize regional standards; and promote social, industrial and economic development and provide consumer protection and human safety by advocating and establishing activities concerning standardization in Africa. ARSO has published over 400 standards. Most of these are adoptions or adaptations of ISO, IEC and Codex standards; there are, however, a few standards that are of interest mainly on the African continent.*

❑ **SADC Cooperation in Standardization (SADCSTAN)**. *The main objective of SADCSTAN is to harmonize standards for products being traded between SADC member States. SADCSTAN member States have agreed to base the SADC harmonized standards on international standards wherever these exist.*

   Members: Angola, Botswana, Democratic Republic of the Congo, Lesotho, Malawi, Mauritius, Mozambique, Namibia, Seychelles, South Africa, Swaziland, United Republic of Tanzania, Zambia, Zimbabwe.

❑ **COMESA Programme on Standardization, Quality Assurance, Metrology and Testing**. *The aim of the programme is to harmonize standards and quality assurance schemes in the COMESA region.*

   Members: Angola, Burundi, Comoros, Democratic Republic of the Congo, Djibouti, Egypt, Eritrea, Ethiopia, Kenya, Madagascar, Malawi, Mauritius, Namibia, Rwanda, Seychelles, Sudan, Swaziland, Uganda, Zambia, Zimbabwe.

❑ **East African Community (Kenya, Uganda and United Republic of Tanzania)**. *The countries belonging to this community have already notified a number of regional standards to other WTO Members under the Agreement on TBT. It has harmonized 383 standards in line with the Metrology, Standards, Testing and Quality Assurance Protocol within the East African Community.*

❑ **Regional Crop Protection Program (RCPP)**. *The programme covers the Comoros, Madagascar, Mauritius, Reunion and Seychelles. These countries have a number of phytosanitary problems in common, such as difficulties in implementing phytosanitary regulations; difficulties in identifying plant pests; and national variations in phytosanitary legislation. Regional solutions to these problems are being sought within the programme.*

CARIBBEAN

❑ **CARICOM Regional Organisation for Standards and Quality (CROSQ)**. *The objectives of CROSQ are to facilitate trade within the CARICOM Single Market and Economy and with other countries; to enhance efficiency and quality in the production of goods and services within CARICOM; and to promote consumer and environmental protection.*

   Trade facilitation is to be realized by promoting the development and harmonization of standards, including metrology, technical regulations and mutual recognition of conformity assessment procedures.

   Members: Antigua and Barbuda, Bahamas, Barbados, Belize, Dominica, Grenada, Guyana, Haiti, Jamaica, Montserrat, Saint Kitts and Nevis, Saint Lucia, Saint Vincent and the Grenadines, Suriname, Trinidad and Tobago.

ASIA

❑ **APEC Sub-Committee on Standards and Conformance (APEC SCSC)**. *The objectives of SCSC are to align members' domestic standards with international standards; to achieve recognition among APEC economies of conformity assessment in regulated and voluntary sectors; to promote cooperation for technical infrastructure development; and to ensure the transparency of the standards and conformity assessments of APEC economies.*

   Members: Australia, Brunei Darussalam, Canada, Chile, China, Hong Kong (China), Indonesia, Japan, Republic of Korea, Malaysia, Mexico, New Zealand, Papua New Guinea, Peru, Philippines, Russian Federation, Singapore, Taiwan Province (China), Thailand, United States, Viet Nam.

➡

❑ *ASEAN Consultative Committee for Standards and Quality (ACCSQ). ASEAN Cooperation on Standards and Conformity Assessment is undertaken mainly through the ASEAN Consultative Committee for Standards and Quality (ACCSQ). The main ACCSQ objective is to facilitate the removal of technical barriers to trade among members, and to expand trade between members and with the rest of the world.*

Members: Brunei Darussalam, Cambodia, Indonesia, Lao People's Democratic Republic, Malaysia, Myanmar, Philippines, Singapore, Thailand, Viet Nam.

ACCSQ tries to harmonize product standards through alignment with international standards; to implement the ASEAN Framework Agreement on mutual recognition agreements (MRAs); to enhance the technical infrastructure and competency in laboratory testing, calibration, certification and accreditation based on internationally accepted procedures and guides; as well as strengthening the information network on standards and technical regulations.

As a general principle, standards are harmonized on a regional basis on the basis of standards adopted at international level by such organizations as ISO, IEC and CAC. This harmonization expedites the process of alignment of national standards to international standards. Regional standards that are not based on international standards are developed only for those agricultural and industrial products which are of importance in intraregional trade, and for which international standards either have not been developed or are not likely to be developed because they are of minor importance in international trade.

In the area of sanitary and phytosanitary measures the work undertaken on a regional basis aims at:

❑ Encouraging cooperation among countries for control of pests and other diseases prevailing in the region;

❑ Harmonizing sanitary and phytosanitary measures at regional level; and

❑ Developing environmentally friendly crop protection measures.

Problems encountered in participating in regional standardization activities

The case studies show that, while countries like Malaysia are able to participate actively in the work of the regional standardization organizations, others encounter problems similar to those they face in participating in international standardization activities. The lack of expertise on the part of the officials participating in the meetings constitutes a major handicap. These difficulties are further accentuated as they are not able to involve industry, the business community and other stakeholders in the preparatory work needed at national level for participation in the work at technical level. In addition, most of these organizations have difficulty providing adequate technical administrative support for work in the area of standardization, because of the financial and other constraints from which they suffer.[8]

However, countries do appear to overcome some of the problems as illustrated below. Work on regional harmonization of standards has been successfully

---

8   Henson et al, *Impact of sanitary and phytosanitary measures on developing countries*, p. 34.

initiated in SADC. The East African Community (Kenya, United Republic of Tanzania and Uganda) has notified a number of regional standards to other WTO Members and is harmonizing standards within the community. CROSQ is making progress in the area of trade facilitation through promotion of development and harmonization of standards, including metrology, technical regulations and mutual recognition of conformity assessment procedures.

Complementary role played by the regional commissions and committees of the international standard-setting organizations

The international standard-setting organizations such as CAC, OIE and IPPC are also actively complementing the work that is being done by the regional standardization bodies, through their regional committees and commissions.

Most of the case study countries appear to be taking interest in the work of these regional committees and commissions. For some of the countries, however, participation suffers from the same limitations that affect their involvement in the international organizations.

Participation in the activities of regional commissions and committees of the international standard-setting organizations and in the activities of the regional standardization bodies would, by improving the knowledge base of the participating officials, improve their capacities for participation in the international standardization activities. Continued and effective participation in regional activities may also gradually prepare countries with a trade interest in a product or a product group to participate more effectively in technical work on formulation of standards at international level.

Need for establishment of regional laboratories and regional service and repair centres

One of the recommendations made by the consultants is that it may be desirable to support the work that is being done at national level, by assisting countries in:

❏ Developing at regional level scientific and technical infrastructure, including laboratory and research facilities; and

❏ Establishing centres for the repair and maintenance of laboratory equipment.

Regional laboratories

The regional laboratories could complement the work done at national level by undertaking basic research that would help exporters in meeting the requirements of technical regulations and sanitary and phytosanitary measures applied to selected products of export interest to countries in the region. One of the areas in which laboratory capacity at regional level may be developed is tissue culture. It is, however, important to recognize that it may not be possible for exporting firms to use such regional laboratories for conformity assessment, as the time taken to transport samples to the laboratory might pose difficulties in the acceptance of results. Such work would have to be undertaken by national laboratories.

Regional centres for repair of test equipment

In some of the countries, where laboratory facilities have been established with the assistance provided under a technical assistance programme, the laboratories are not functioning well because of the non-existence of facilities in the country for servicing and repair of the specialized equipment. In most cases, the laboratories have to send the equipment to countries where manufacturers of the equipment are located. To overcome this problem, it may be necessary to consider whether it would be possible to persuade manufacturers supplying the equipment to establish joint service facilities in the region.

Problems experienced by the case study countries in complying with technical regulations and sanitary and phytosanitary measures of importing markets

General

As noted in chapter 1, technical regulations providing mandatory quality and safety requirements for products are applied by countries to a relatively narrow range of products. These include machinery and equipment (such as boilers, electricity-driven tools and food processing equipment), and raw materials and agricultural inputs (such as fertilizers and insecticides). Consumer articles to which such regulations apply include electrical appliances and information technology products, pharmaceuticals, cosmetics, and toys. For most of these products, the case study countries other than Malaysia are mainly importers. Their exports of these products are at present extremely limited. The case studies have, therefore, found that exporters from these countries do not encounter any major difficulties in marketing their products because of the technical regulations applicable in their main export markets.

Some of these countries appear, however, to have encountered problems in complying with labelling requirements for food and other consumer products. Exporters from Jamaica, for instance, have complained about United States food labelling requirements; the design and positioning of labels, and the cost of obtaining approval for their use, pose serious problems in exporting to that market. Mauritian exporters have found that their exports to France of preserved fruits and vegetables are sometimes rejected on the grounds that labelling requirements are not fully met.

All the case study countries appear to face problems in complying with sanitary and phytosanitary measures. The products affected include fresh fruits and vegetables, flowers and other horticultural products, fish and fish products, meat and meat products, and other processed food products. Box 13 provides a synoptic picture of importing countries in which barriers are encountered in some of these product sectors.

In the sections that follow, a few examples have been provided from the case studies to illustrate the type of problems which are being encountered, and the efforts that are being made to find solutions to these problems.

Box 13
Problems experienced by case study countries due to the application of sanitary and phytosanitary measures by importing region/country

EXPORTING COUNTRIES	IMPORTING REGION/COUNTRY							
	EU	United States	Japan	Australia	Republic of Korea	Kenya	South Africa	Switzerland
Fish and fish products								
Jamaica	X							
Kenya	X							
Malaysia	X							
Mauritius	X							
Namibia	X							
Uganda	X							
Horticultural products								
Jamaica		X						
Kenya	X			X			X	
Malaysia	X	X	X	X	X			
Mauritius	X		X					
Namibia		X						
Uganda	X	X	X					
Meat and poultry								
Jamaica								
Kenya		X						
Malaysia	X			X				
Mauritius	X					X		
Namibia	X							X
Uganda								
Processed food products								
Jamaica	X	X						
Kenya								
Malaysia	X		X					
Mauritius							X	
Namibia								

Water treatment, fumigation and other requirements for control of pests or diseases

Legislation in some countries requires that a country wishing to export fresh fruits and vegetables to them must obtain prior approval from the appropriate authorities, before it can commence exports. Such approval is granted if the authorities are satisfied that the fruits are free from diseases and pests not existing in the importing country. Jamaica, for instance, has not been able to get approval for its exports of mangoes as the United States considers that West Indian and Caribbean fruit flies are present in the fruit. The United States may allow imports if mangoes are subject to hot water treatment. No such facility, however, exists at present in Jamaica.

A number of other countries – Australia, Japan and the Republic of Korea included – also exercise strict control over imports of fresh fruits, vegetables and flowers to prevent entry of exotic plant pests and diseases. Imports of such products are prohibited unless prior approval is obtained or a specific treatment given to the produce before export. Australia, for instance, requires glyphosate devitalization of flower shipments before entry into the country.

Problems posed by Maximum Residue Limits (MRLs)

The case studies reveal that countries are facing problems in complying with the rules adopted by importing countries limiting the maximum levels of pesticides and other residues (MRLs) in fresh fruits and vegetables. Developing countries often find it difficult to comply with these requirements, as many of them do not have legislation requiring prior approval of fertilizers and pesticides that are marketed in the country. This results in fertilizers and pesticides that are prohibited from use in importing countries being used in production of crops intended for export. Farmers are also often influenced into making excessive use of pesticides, in order to ensure that exports of fresh fruits and vegetables are not banned by importing countries because of the presence of pests and diseases.

Of particular concern in this regard is the decision by the EU to set import tolerances for pesticide residues for as many as 100 chemical ingredients to zero (i.e. the level of detection) as from July 2003. Exporters of fresh fruits and vegetables from a number of developing countries are apprehensive that complying with these requirements may pose them serious problems. There would be also increasing demands on laboratories in developing countries for analysis of the residues, to ensure before exporting that tolerance levels are met. In a number of countries such laboratory facilities do not exist or are inadequate.

Inspection of processing facilities by inspectors from importing countries

Imports of fish and fish products and of meat and meat products are allowed by some developed countries only if they are produced and processed at facilities that have sanitary conditions equivalent to those prescribed for processing of such products in their territories. These countries further undertake inspections, to assess the extent to which exporting countries comply with these requirements, by sending their national inspectors. The costs of such inspection are to be met by the exporting firms. Such requirements are considered necessary by the importing countries, in order to ensure that imported products meet cleanliness and other hygiene standards that they apply to their domestic producers. In practice, however, they pose serious problems of compliance for exporting firms from developing countries, particularly as the requirements prescribed by the regulations or measures in the importing countries are different from those applicable in the exporting country.

Fish and fish products

The case studies contain detailed information on the problems encountered by Jamaica, Kenya and Uganda in exporting fish and fish products to the European Union as a result of the application of such measures. Fish processing units from Jamaica, for instance, have pointed out that they experience considerable difficulties in complying with the requirements of the EU directives regarding water control, pest and vermin control, and other general conditions regarding maintenance practices, as they are different from the standards applied in Jamaica. Uganda's fish exports to the EU were stopped in 1998 because of the presence of cholera and standards that were assessed as not meeting EU requirements. The relevant EU directive is the prime norm for Uganda's fish exporters, and exports of fish have resumed since compliance with the EU directive was re-established. Exporting units from Kenya are facing difficulties in complying with the requirements in the EU directives because of the limited storage facilities for fish and fish products at places where fish is harvested, and inadequate laboratory facilities for ensuring that the requirements imposed by the directives are fully met.

Ackee

Because of the presence of hypoglycin (a toxin present in unripe ackee), since October 1999 the Jamaican authorities have been required to implement a system of prior approval and regulation of ackee processors wanting to export ackee to the United States.

Meat and meat products

The inability of abattoirs in Mauritius to meet the standards prescribed by the EU is preventing them from exporting venison and chicken to Reunion, an island country which is part of France and so a member of the EU. Norway requires meat imported from Namibia to be tested in abattoirs and factories in Namibia and again after importation into Norway.

Cheese and cheese products

Processing facilities in Jamaica have not been able to get approval for export to the EU of cheese produced from curds imported from New Zealand.

Registration and prior clearance requirements

Registration and prior clearance requirements, which are applied by some countries, could also pose difficulties for exporters by adding to costs. The United States, for instance, requires exporters of packaged food products to file with the United States Food and Drug Administration full details of their production process before they are permitted access to the United States market. Furthermore, producers of low-acid and acidified canned food are required to obtain prior approval of their product and production process. A significant number of product consignments from Jamaica has been barred from entering the United States market, as importers have not been able to produce the required documentation.

Ironically, measures taken by importing countries to facilitate imports could also act as barriers to trade, if the cost of such measures is, in the long run passed on to exporters. A case in point is the decision by the United States to post officers from the Phytosanitary Unit of its Agriculture Department as resident officers in Jamaica for 'pre-clearance of fresh fruits and vegetables'. This facilitates the speedy clearance of goods through United States Customs without further inspections after importation. In the initial period, the cost of the pre-clearance programme was met by USAID under its assistance programme. Following the termination of this assistance, the Jamaican Government is now meeting the cost of the programme (including the salaries of the United States officials) by imposing a 'per box' levy on all products exported. Though the pre-clearance system ensures that imported goods are cleared by United States Customs without delay on their arrival in the country and that there are no rejections, the service results in additional costs to exporters.

Application of standards that are higher than the international standards

The case studies show that some of the problems faced by developing countries arise from the application by developed countries, in their sanitary and phytosanitary measures, of standards that are higher than the international standards. In some cases, these sanitary and phytosanitary measures impose additional obligations which are not stipulated in the international standards.

An example is that of Japanese legislation, which does not permit the use of some food additives that are considered safe by international standards. Furthermore, the approval of food additives is highly product-specific; benzoic acid is approved for use in soy sauce but not in curry sauce.

Examples in the case studies of requirements which are additional to those specified in the international standards are the requirements of the EU and the United States for prior inspection and approval of abattoirs where meat is produced, and the EU requirements for inspection and approval of fish and fish processing units by its inspectors or by the local competent authority.

The case studies also refer to complaints by exporters in some of the case study countries that the sanitary and phytosanitary measures are often applied to imported products more rigorously than they are applied to domestically produced products. Such cases may arise where imported products are considered to present more risk from a health safety point of view than domestic products.

Problems encountered in trade with other developing countries

From the information available in the case studies, it would appear that developing countries are also encountering problems as a result of the application of sanitary and phytosanitary measures by other developing countries. The case study of Mauritius refers to the ban by Kenya on imports of 'day-old chicks' from the country because of concern about the disease

Avian encephalomyelitis. According to Mauritius documentation, the ban was imposed without testing of the imported products or an assessment of the risk the disease presented to human health. The ban was, however, subsequently removed. Mauritius has also encountered problems in complying with South Africa's food safety requirements for canned tuna fish, as inspection and test certificates issued by Mauritian authorities are not acceptable to the South African authorities. ITC organized a mission in February 2002 to inspect the local company to see if it could meet the food standards of the South African Bureau of Standards and to assist in negotiating a technical agreement between the South African Bureau of Standards and the corresponding regulatory authority in Mauritius. The short-term outcome was that canned tuna would be accepted in South Africa subject to the condition that each consignment be inspected. In the longer term the Department of Veterinary Services of Mauritius would have to be accredited as an inspection body and the food laboratory of the Mauritius Standards Bureau would have to be accredited as a testing laboratory.

Trade among developing countries constitutes a high proportion of international trade today. A number of these countries are now taking action for further promotion and development of trade, by forming regional economic groupings and gradually reducing tariffs on imports from countries in the region.

As tariffs applicable to imports from countries in the region fall, the exporters from these countries may find that the technical regulations and the sanitary and phytosanitary measures adopted by developing countries to which they export, constitute one of the major barriers to trade. In practice, it may be difficult for exporting and importing countries to resolve problems that may arise on the basis of the provisions of the Agreement on TBT, because in a large number of developing countries, a high percentage of the technical regulations applied are not based on international standards (see chapter 6). In relation to sanitary and phytosanitary measures, even though Codex standards appear to have been adopted, their enforcement at domestic level is generally lax. If an exporting country complains that a measure not based on an international standard is causing an unnecessary barrier to its trade, the country maintaining the measure must, under the rules of the Agreement on SPS, justify its application on the basis of risk assessment. Most of the developing countries maintaining such measures do not have at present the scientific personnel and laboratory facilities that are required for undertaking such risk assessment. Undertaking such assessment involves large financial outlay; most developing countries would not be able to find the resources required for this purpose.

Moreover, practical problems of the type faced by Mauritius in its trade with South Africa are likely to be faced by a number of other developing countries, as in many of these countries the institutional framework needed for accreditation of authorities responsible for inspection and of laboratories responsible for testing is yet to be developed. In this situation, importing developing countries would be reluctant to rely on the inspections and tests carried out in the exporting countries to meet the requirements of their technical regulations and sanitary and phytosanitary measures. As a result, many of them may require that products certified by authorities which are not properly accredited must undergo further inspections and tests after importation.

CHAPTER 6

Progress made in adopting administrative arrangements for the implementation of the Agreements on TBT and SPS and in abiding by their obligations

General

The previous chapter provided an overview of the difficulties faced by the case study countries in complying with the technical regulations and sanitary and phytosanitary measures that are applied by countries to which their present exports are directed. This chapter assesses:

❑ *How far the case study countries have been able to build up the institutional and legal framework that is required for the implementation of the Agreements on TBT and SPS;*

❑ *Progress made in implementing the provisions relating to the establishment of enquiry points and those imposing obligations to notify to the WTO Secretariat products in respect of which new technical regulations and sanitary and phytosanitary measures not based on international standards are being adopted;*

❑ *Progress made in accordance with the objectives of the two Agreements in achieving alignment of national standards to international standards and in basing technical regulations and sanitary and phytosanitary measures on international standards; and*

❑ *Progress made in developing systems for accreditation of laboratories and inspection bodies responsible for conformity assessment.*

This is followed by an assessment of the extent to which the capacities required for the application of technical regulations and for the enforcement of sanitary and phytosanitary measures at customs borders have been fully developed.

Administrative arrangements for the implementation of the Agreements on TBT and SPS

In all six countries covered by the case studies, the ministry handling WTO-related work is also responsible for coordinating work relating to the implementation of the Agreements on TBT and SPS. The Agreement on TBT further calls on members to encourage their national standard-setting bodies to accept the 'Code of Good Practice for the Preparation, Adoption and Application of Standards'. The Code urges standardization bodies to base the standards that they formulate, to the maximum extent possible, on international standards. The standardization bodies in the six case study countries have accepted the Code.

The approach adopted by the focal ministry in each country for coordination of work relating to the Agreements on TBT and SPS, however, shows some variations. In Kenya, Malaysia, Mauritius and Uganda the responsibility for coordinating work among different ministries and other interested stakeholders (e.g. regulatory authorities, industry and trade associations, chambers of commerce and consumer associations) is with a committee established by the ministry that serves as a focal point for all WTO work. This committee is generally responsible for overseeing the implementation of all WTO Agreements. However, in some countries, such as Malaysia and Mauritius, there are specific committees for SPS and/or TBT. The case study for Jamaica mentions that it was acknowledged that there was a certain amount of overlap and fragmentation with respect to the responsibility of the various authorities and a proposal for a coordinating committee has been floated. In the case of Namibia, no formal institutional arrangements for coordination of work among different ministries in WTO-related areas, either on an overall basis or in relation to the two Agreements, appear to have been established. The country has further informed the WTO Secretariat that all TBT-related standardization and quality assurance work in Namibia is handled by the South African Bureau of Standards.

The consultants did not have time to assess how far the institutional mechanisms that have been established are effective in securing the involvement of all stakeholders in evolving policies to be followed in the discussions at international level on trade-related standardization issues. The general impression is that, except in the case of Malaysia, there is a considerable need for improvement in the coordination of work among different ministries. In the area of sanitary and phytosanitary measures, for instance, in a number of these countries, the responsibility for work is often fragmented among the ministries of health and agriculture and the departments responsible for animal husbandry and veterinary control. It is also important to note, in this context, that while an appropriate institutional framework is essential, the level and effectiveness of coordination depends largely on the willingness of officials from different ministries to share responsibilities. If such willingness does not exist, efforts made in improving and strengthening of the institutional mechanism do not produce the desired results.

A related issue is the effectiveness of non-governmental participation in these coordination meetings. Even though the representatives of trade and industry participate in the meetings that are arranged, their contribution to the discussions is often limited, because of a lack of awareness on their part either of the objectives and rules of the two Agreements or of the important role that international standards play in facilitating international trade.

Transparency obligations

In order to ensure the transparency of technical regulations and sanitary and phytosanitary measures that are being applied or are under preparation, the two Agreements impose on member countries obligations to:

❑ Establish enquiry points; and

❑ Notify to the WTO Secretariat products for which new regulations or measures[9] are being formulated immediately after the regulations or measures are published at national level in draft form.

---

9   If they are not based on international standards and may have a significant effect on trade.

Enquiry points

The Agreement on TBT calls on countries to establish an enquiry point from which interested member countries can obtain information on technical regulations, conformity assessment procedures, national and regional standards and bilateral arrangements for mutual recognition of conformity assessment. The Agreement on SPS imposes a similar obligation in respect of sanitary and phytosanitary measures.

Box 14 lists the agencies that have been designated as enquiry points in the six case study countries. The Agreement on TBT lays down that each member country should ensure that there is one enquiry point; however, for legal or administrative reasons, more than one enquiry point can be established. The Agreement on SPS requires that each member should ensure that there is one enquiry point. In the case of technical regulations, all the case study countries have established one enquiry point as required by the Agreement; in the case of sanitary and phytosanitary measures, some of them have established three separate enquiry points – e.g. in Kenya, the Director of Agriculture in the Ministry of Agriculture and Rural Development has been designated as the enquiry point for information on plant health matters, the Director of Veterinary Services in the Ministry of Agriculture and Rural Development for information on veterinary matters, and the Director of Medical Services in the Ministry of Health for information on human health matters.

The enquiry points in some of the case study countries appear to be working reasonably well, and are able to meet promptly and effectively the requests for information from interested exporters and importers as well as to respond to the questions received from other governments.

In some countries, such as Namibia, financial constraints appear to inhibit governments from allocating the full budgetary resources required for effective operation of the enquiry points.

Notification obligations

Requirement for notification of proposed technical regulations or sanitary and phytosanitary measures

The Agreements on TBT and SPS require countries to send notifications to the WTO Secretariat of products for which they propose to adopt technical regulations, sanitary and phytosanitary measures, and procedures for conformity assessment, in all cases where they are not based on international standards and may have a significant effect on trade. Such notification is to be made as soon as the drafts are published for comments, and at least two months before their application on a mandatory basis. The purpose of the notification system is to bring the drafts to the attention of other member countries, and through them their industry and business associations, and to provide an opportunity to comment on them. This is to ensure that the product specifications applied and the process and production methods used in other member countries are adequately taken into account by the notifying country in adopting final regulations or measures.

As soon as it receives notifications, the WTO Secretariat transmits them to the member countries. These are circulated to relevant government departments which are in turn expected to transmit them to the industry and business associations in the country and solicit their comments. The two Agreements put obligations on countries formulating such regulations to take into account the comments received within the stipulated time of two months. Where urgent problems of safety, health, national protection or national security arise for a

Box 14
Agencies designated as enquiry points

Country	Agreement on TBT	Agreement on SPS
Jamaica	Jamaica Bureau of Standards.	Plant Quarantine/Plant Inspection Unit, Ministry of Agriculture.
Kenya	Kenya Bureau of Standards.	Director of Medical Services, Ministry of Health (human health). Director of Agriculture, Ministry of Agriculture and Rural Development (plant health). Director of Veterinary Services, Ministry of Agriculture and Rural Development (animal health).
Malaysia	Standards and Industrial Research Institute of Malaysia Berhad.	Department of Agriculture, Ministry of Agriculture (plant products). Food Quality Control Department, Ministry of Health (food safety). Department of Veterinary Services, Ministry of Agriculture (animals and animal products).
Mauritius	Mauritius Standards Bureau.	Division of Plant Pathology and Quarantine, Ministry of Agriculture.
Namibia	Namibian Standards Information and Quality Office.	Directorate of Planning, Ministry of Agriculture, Water and Rural Development (general issues). Chief Veterinary Office, Ministry of Agriculture, Water and Rural Development (zoosanitary issues). Directorate of Extension and Engineering, Ministry of Agriculture, Water and Rural Development (phytosanitary and CAC issues).
Uganda	Uganda National Bureau of Standards.	Uganda National Bureau of Standards. Plant Protection Area, Ministry of Agriculture, Animal Industry and Fisheries (phytosanitary matters). Animal Health Area, Ministry of Agriculture, Animal Industry and Fisheries (zoosanitary issues).

WTO Member, the two-month period can be shortened. Notifications received by the WTO Secretariat can also be downloaded from the WTO website – the National Enquiry Point of Kenya follows this procedure.

The experience of the case study countries with regard to the notification systems is described below. This is followed by an overview of the extent to which the provisions relating to notification are being implemented by developing countries when adopting new technical regulations or sanitary and phytosanitary measures.

Circulation of notifications received from WTO

The situation regarding the circulation of notifications received from WTO to industry and business associations differs from country to country.

There is an established and functional system for circulation of TBT notifications in Malaysia, Kenya and Jamaica, whereas TBT notifications are not circulated to stakeholders in Mauritius, Namibia and Uganda. Notifications from WTO about sanitary and phytosanitary measures are circulated to relevant stakeholders in Jamaica, Kenya, Malaysia, and Mauritius whereas they are not circulated in Namibia and Uganda.

Box 15
Authorities responsible for making notifications to WTO under the Agreements on TBT and SPS

Country	Designated authority	Number of notifications*
Agreement on TBT		
Jamaica	Ministry of Foreign Affairs and Foreign Trade.	30
Kenya	Director of External Trade, Ministry of Commerce and Industry.	-
Malaysia	Standards and Industrial Research Institute of Malaysia.	165
Mauritius	Ministry of Industry and International Trade.	-
Namibia	No clear procedure for domestic notifications.	-
Uganda	Ministry of Tourism, Trade and Industry.	-
Agreement on SPS		
Jamaica	Plant Quarantine/Produce Inspector, Ministry of Agriculture.	5 (3)
Kenya	Department of External Trade, Ministry of Commerce and Industry.	2 (1)
Malaysia	Department of Veterinary Services, Ministry of Agriculture.	11 (6)
Mauritius	Division of Plant Pathology and Quarantine, Ministry of Agriculture.	9 (5)
Namibia	Ministry of Trade and Industry.	-
Uganda	Ministry of Tourism, Trade and Industry.	1

*The number in brackets indicates notifications about emergency measures.

In a number of cases, countries have not been able to take advantage of the notification procedures to comment on the drafts of technical regulations or sanitary and phytosanitary measures. This could be attributed to two factors. First, with the increasing attention being paid in most countries, particularly developed countries, to protecting consumer interests and to food safety, the number of notifications circulated by WTO for comments is on the increase. Second, because of resource constraints and lack of expertise, it is difficult to sort out the notifications and circulate them to interested parties.

Notifications by the case study countries

All case study countries have designated authorities that are responsible for notifying to WTO the products for which technical regulations or sanitary and phytosanitary measures not based on international standards are being adopted. The authorities are listed in box 15. In the case of sanitary and phytosanitary measures, these authorities are also responsible for notifying to WTO any emergency measures taken to restrict or prohibit imports.

Many of the case study countries appear to have established procedures requiring ministries and regulatory authorities to transmit the draft regulations or measures to the designated authorities, so that they can be transmitted by them to the WTO Secretariat for circulation to all member countries. Out of the six countries, four have made no notifications in the area of technical regulations, even though they appear to have adopted mandatory standards that are not based on international standards. More notifications have been made in the area of sanitary and phytosanitary measures; the majority of these are emergency measures to restrict or prohibit imports.

In accordance with article 15.2 of the Agreement on TBT, WTO Members should inform the WTO Committee on TBT about measures taken to ensure the implementation and administration of the Agreement. All the case study countries except Kenya have done this.

Progress made in aligning national standards to international standards and basing technical regulations or sanitary and phytosanitary measures on international standards

One of the aims of the Agreements on TBT and SPS is to ensure that technical regulations or sanitary and phytosanitary measures formulated and applied by countries do not constitute barriers to trade, by aligning the regulations and measures to international standards. The question which arises is how far developing countries have been able to align their national standards to international standards.

Alignment of national standards to international standards

Industrial products

A recent study[10] by ISO on the problems faced 'by the standardization bodies and other stakeholders from developing countries' found that in 70 per cent of the countries less than 50 per cent of the national standards were identical to international standards. In the remaining countries covered by the study, the percentage was significantly lower.

What are the reasons for the lack of progress in aligning national standards to international standards?

According to the study, the main reason for the reluctance of these countries to pursue work on the alignment of their national standards to international standards is that they have not been able to participate in the work on formulating the relevant international standards. They therefore remain unsure of the extent to which the international standards are suitable for use by their industries. The study mentions other reasons for such reluctance, such as lack of funds at the level of national standard-setting bodies and in industry, lack of awareness of the need for such alignment, and lack of expertise in standardization.

---

10   Participation of developing countries in international standardization: Background paper presented to ISO General Assembly Workshop, Stockholm, 24 September 2002 (page 21).

These findings are further confirmed by the case studies. A few of the international standards are also considered unsuitable for adoption because of climatic conditions: the required environmental criteria specified for testing are suitable only for temperate zone countries and not for countries in the tropical region, where temperatures remain high.

Agricultural products

The ISO study covers broadly the standards prepared by ISO, which apply largely to industrial products. The situation in relation to the standards applied to agricultural products appears to be different. In most of the case study countries, national standards, both voluntary and mandatory, applied to food products appear to be based on Codex standards.

Use of international standards in technical regulations and sanitary and phytosanitary measures

Technical regulations

A related question that arises is how far the technical regulations or sanitary and phytosanitary measures adopted by developing countries are based on international standards. In 61 per cent of the countries covered by the ISO study referred to earlier, more than half of the technical regulations were not based on international standards. What is further revealing is that, in 59 per cent of the countries in the study, more than half of the technical regulations were not even based on national standards. The study attributes the latter situation to the lack of cooperation between standardizing bodies and the ministries and agencies responsible for formulating technical regulations.

Sanitary and phytosanitary measures

On the whole, there appears to be greater recognition of the need to use international standards as a basis for sanitary and phytosanitary measures. For example, Malaysia and Mauritius, which are substantial importers of food and have a well-developed food control system, use all relevant Codex standards as the basis for the standards prescribed in their national legislation. On the other hand, Namibia, which is also a substantial food importer, does not appear to have a well-developed food control system, except for control of meat products to ensure freedom from foot and mouth disease. Namibia still relies on South African standards.

Similarly, OIE standards and codes provide the basis for national standards for animal health in all case study countries. For practical reasons, however, several of the countries find it difficult to maintain effective animal health regimes.

The situation with respect to plant health standards appears somewhat different. To date, the norms established by IPPC have tended to relate to definitions and concepts, methods and methodology, and administrative procedures rather than to control of specific pest risks. In part, this reflects the fact that IPPC did not perform the role of establishing international standards until the mid-1990s and is still in the early stages of its standard-setting programme. However, it also reflects the fact that pest and disease problems differ markedly between countries.

Progress made in accreditation of laboratories, inspection bodies and certification bodies

For a number of products, importing countries do not consider manufacturers' declarations of conformity sufficient, and require imported products to be accompanied by a certificate of conformity assessment issued by a properly accredited laboratory, inspection body or certification body. Though most of the case study countries appear to have laboratories and inspection bodies that carry out tests and inspections in order to assess conformity, only Malaysia has effective systems for their accreditation by a recognized national accreditation body: SIRIM QAS provides inspection services and audits on behalf of foreign certification bodies and purchasers. There are several arrangements, at certification body and accreditation body level, between organizations in Malaysia and those in other countries. If the situation in the other case studies is taken as illustrative of the situation in many of the other developing countries, it appears that most of them will need assistance to establish national accreditation bodies or to have their conformity assessment bodies accredited by a foreign accreditation body or by a regional accreditation body.[11]

Capacities for ensuring that imported goods conform to regulations and measures

All the case study countries appear to have established mechanisms at their customs borders to ensure that imported products meet the standards prescribed in their technical regulations and sanitary and phytosanitary measures. Their effectiveness in preventing imports of goods that do not meet prescribed standards or are sub-standard depends, however, on the efficiency with which customs and other administrative departments apply the border control measures, and the availability of laboratory facilities and trained personnel to undertake inspections and carry out tests.

From this perspective, as regards sanitary and phytosanitary measures, Malaysia appears to have an effective system for control at the border. Mauritius requires that no new food product should be sold in the country unless prior approval is obtained. Kenyan regulations require all imported products for which Kenyan standards do not exist to conform to the standards prevailing in the exporting country.

The case studies suggest, however, that the capacities for ensuring that imported products meet requirements prescribed by SPS measures need considerable strengthening and improvement in a number of countries.

---

11   Currently there is no operational regional accreditation body.

CHAPTER 7

Technical assistance: identified needs and suggested delivery mechanism

Recommendations and observations in the joint report of the consultants

The consultants, who had worked separately on the case studies, also submitted a joint report giving their views on the strengths and weaknesses of existing technical assistance programmes and on how these programmes could be strengthened and oriented to make them more responsive to the needs of developing countries, taking into account the stage reached by them in standardization development. Appendix I[12] contains extracts from the report covering these issues. In considering the nature and type of assistance that could be provided in the area of technical regulations and sanitary and phytosanitary measures, it is necessary to bear in mind some of the observations made and views expressed by the consultants in their joint report. Important among these are the following:

❑ Though considerable financial resources were being devoted by donor countries for providing assistance in the area of technical regulations and sanitary and phytosanitary measures, either directly under their bilateral assistance programmes or by making funds available to international standard-setting organizations and other international organizations, the amount devoted fell far short of the total requirements for assistance by developing countries. As an illustration, the consultants pointed out that in one of the case study countries 'technical assistance amounting to US$ 6 million was agreed upon by donors, but eventually only US$ 3 million was provided'. Moreover, in respect of the amount actually allocated, there was a time lag between the approval and its delivery. Because of this, the consultants observed that there was a sense of frustration in certain case study countries, and a view was developing that their problems were not being taking seriously.

❑ Assistance required in the area of technical regulations and sanitary and phytosanitary measures was of a highly technical nature. The agencies in developed countries responsible for providing assistance on a bilateral basis did not always have the capacity to evaluate proposals for assistance. The result was that in many cases the assistance provided did not reflect the needs and priorities of the recipient countries.

❑ In many cases, training was being provided on the application of technical regulations and the enforcement of sanitary and phytosanitary measures, without countries being provided with the financial resources to establish laboratory facilities and acquire testing equipment. In other cases,

12   For details see pp. 83–95.

sophisticated laboratory equipment was provided, even though the recipient country did not have the skilled human resources to make use of it. Technical assistance related to training has not always been effective.

❑ As many of the projects for capacity building did not always insist on a contribution from the recipient countries, there was often a lack of commitment on the part of the governments of the aid-receiving countries to support and continue the work after the initial infrastructure was established with aid money.

❑ There was also a need for greater coordination among donor countries, and between donor countries and international organizations (both standardization and others), in providing technical assistance to developing countries.

In this context, it is important to note that major steps towards establishing coordination in providing assistance in the field of standardization, particularly in the area of food safety, plant and animal health and other areas covered by sanitary and phytosanitary measures, have been taken by WTO, the World Bank, FAO, WHO and OIE. These organizations have established a trust fund to administer the Standards and Development Facility, which will, *inter alia*, assist developing countries in the development or improvement of national food safety, animal and plant health systems.

Specific areas in which technical assistance is needed

General

The specific areas in which technical assistance is needed include:

❑ Improving the participation of developing countries in standardization activities at international and regional levels, particularly in the work at technical level on formulation of draft standards for products of export interest to them;

❑ Creating greater awareness among industry and trade associations of the need to take a more active interest in standardization activities at both national and international level;

❑ On request, helping developing countries to meet the requirements of technical regulations and sanitary and phytosanitary measures applicable in their export markets;

❑ Assisting interested developing countries to establish systems for alerting exporters to forthcoming changes in technical regulations or sanitary and phytosanitary measures; and

❑ On request, helping developing countries to establish bodies, at national or regional level, for accreditation of conformity assessment bodies, or to access the services of foreign accreditation bodies.

In developing technical assistance programmes in each of the above areas, it is necessary to ensure that the assistance provided:

❑ Takes into account the fact that the technical assistance needs of developing countries vary considerably from country to country, according to the stage reached by them in the development of their standardization infrastructure. Consequently the assistance provided has to be tailored according to the needs of individual countries.

❑ Is transparent and does not result in duplication of the assistance provided by donor countries under their bilateral assistance programmes or by international standard-setting organizations and other international organizations.

Assistance aimed at improving the participation of developing countries in standardization activities at international level

The analysis in the case studies has clearly brought out that the major problem encountered by developing countries, particularly those considered as less advanced (on the basis of the stage reached by them in the development of the standardization and conformity assessment infrastructure), is lack of human resources. Most of them do not have personnel available in the national standard-setting bodies, or in the ministries and government departments that are responsible for participation in international or regional standardization activities, with knowledge and expertise in the specific scientific fields related to the products for which standards are being formulated.

Several mechanisms for improving the participation of developing countries in international standardization activities have been adopted by international standard-setting organizations themselves, and others are being considered. Box 16 summarizes their strengths and weaknesses.

It will be noticed that, although all of these mechanisms are steps in the right direction, they are mainly directed to facilitating attendance at meetings by covering travel costs or to overcoming problems caused by financial constraints. With the exception of two mechanisms discussed later, their direct contribution to assisting developing countries to overcome the basic problem of lack of technical expertise is at best marginal.

For instance, the right to comment by e-mail would benefit only countries with the required expertise available in the field to which the standard relates, but who are constrained from taking an active interest in the work at international or regional level because of the lack of financial resources to meet travel and other expenditures. Its usefulness for countries that do not have such expertise, which is generally the case for most of the countries in the case studies, would be extremely limited. There are even risks that the lack of expertise might result in a country making comments or providing support to proposals for modifications suggested by other countries that were not necessarily in the interest of its own industries.

Likewise, proposals for developing countries to co-host with a developed country the secretariat of a technical committee, or co-chair it, could lead to its improved participation in the work on formulation of standards if it had the required expertise and the facilities needed at national level to carry out the supporting analysis and research. Consequently, the adoption of any such proposal would provide an advantage only to those few developing countries that have expertise in the field but are constrained from offering host facilities because of lack of financial resources.

From this and the analysis in box 16, it would appear that only two mechanisms appear to have potential for assisting developing countries in overcoming to some extent the problems that they encounter as a result of the lack of expertise. These are technical workshops prior to technical committee meetings, and mentoring and twinning arrangements, both of which are described below.

Box 16

Strengths and weaknesses of the mechanisms under consideration in international standardization and other organizations for improving developing country participation in the standard-setting process

Mechanism	Strengths and weaknesses
• *Financial assistance to attend meetings:* – *Payment of special allowance by organization;* – *Sponsorship by developed countries.*	**Strength** • *Creating awareness of the work done by the organization.* **Weaknesses** • *Does not address problems arising from lack of technical/scientific experience of officials attending the technical level meetings of technical committees.* • *Donor countries may expect support from sponsored developing countries to their proposals for changes and modifications to the draft standards.*
• *Submission of comments on draft standards by e-mail.* • *Reform of voting procedures to include postal/electronic voting.*	**Strength** • *Enables countries to participate in work at technical level without incurring expenditure on travel.* **Weakness** • *Not useful if the officials commenting do not have the expertise required for making comments.*
• *More equitable sharing of right to host secretariat of technical committees between developed and developing countries.* • *Having developing countries act as co-hosts of secretariats of technical committees and as co-chairpersons.*	**Strength** • *Create greater interest on the part of developing countries in participating in technical level meetings.* **Weakness** • *Financial costs may inhibit countries from offering host facilities for secretariat or acting as co-hosts.*
• *Holding workshops prior to the meetings of technical committees.*	**Strengths** • *Facilitates attendance at technical committee meetings.* • *Improves understanding of the standard and of the proposals made for changes and modifications.* **Weakness** • *Does not address the problems arising from the lack of technical/scientific experience of officials attending the technical level meetings.*
• *Mentoring and twinning arrangements.*	**Strengths** • *Addresses the problems arising from the lack of technical/scientific experience of officials attending technical level meetings.* • *Ensures that assistance provided is needs-based.* **Weakness** • *The effectiveness of the assistance provided is influenced greatly by the willingness of the mentoring countries to provide assistance.*

Sources: Spencer Henson et al, *Review of Developing Country Needs and Involvement in International Standards-Setting Bodies*, February 2001 (monograph), pp. 83–91; and observations in the case studies.

Workshops prior to meetings of technical committees

First is the mechanism of holding technical assistance workshops for officials from developing countries for three to four days prior to the meetings of the technical committees. This improves the participants' understanding of issues under discussion in the relevant technical committees. It also facilitates attendance at meetings of the committees, as travel costs for coming to the workshop are met from technical assistance funds.

Broadly speaking, the responsibility for arranging workshops prior to the meetings of technical committees would rest with the international standard-setting organizations responsible for the formulation of standards.

Mentoring and twinning arrangements: their objectives and purpose

The second mechanism, which could contribute significantly to alleviating the problems faced by developing countries because of the lack of expertise, aims at encouraging them to enter into what have come to be known as 'mentoring and twinning arrangements'. The initiative could be taken both by the international standard-setting organizations and by other international organizations.

The dictionary meaning of the term 'mentor' is 'experienced and trusted adviser'. 'Twinning' is a process by which similar materials or bodies are brought together. The term 'mentoring and twinning arrangement' is therefore applied to an arrangement under which a country with the technical capacity to provide assistance in particular fields agrees to provide assistance to a country or countries that are in need of it.

The international organizations play the role of coordinator and catalyst, by bringing together countries that can act as 'mentors' and provide advice and 'twinning' them with countries that need assistance. The actual areas of assistance, and the terms and conditions on which it will be provided, are left to be negotiated on a bilateral basis or a plurilateral basis between the interested mentor country and the country or countries wishing to obtain assistance.

The main advantages of the arrangements are twofold. First, the assistance provided is, from the point of view of countries receiving it, needs-based. Second, countries have an opportunity to shop around and select the mentor country that is best equipped to provide the type of assistance they need.

Need to establish a forum to encourage countries to enter into mentoring and twinning arrangements, where feasible, on a South-South basis

A forum for negotiating mentoring and twinning arrangements, where feasible, on a South-South basis, should be established for the following reasons:

❑ First, the establishment of a mechanism for mentoring and twinning arrangements would further highlight the need to take practical measures to ensure improved participation of developing countries in international standardization activities, in order to ensure that the standards adopted do not pose problems of compliance for them and that adoption by the trading partners of developing countries does not result in the creation of unnecessary barriers to trade.

❑ Second, although the primary focus of the mechanism would be on the provision of assistance needed to improve participation in international standardization activities, the framework established could also be used to provide assistance on other trade-related aspects of standardization and conformity assessment work. The areas in which mentor countries could provide such assistance include:

  – Assistance in formulating technical regulations and sanitary and phytosanitary measures and enforcing them;

  – Assistance in establishing accreditation bodies responsible for accreditation of laboratories and other conformity assessment bodies;

  – Practical training of officials from twinning countries in the standardization area in which they need such assistance, by seconding them to work in the standardization institutions in the mentoring countries;

- Making available to requesting countries services of technical personnel with expertise in the scientific field of the standards under formulation; and

- Assistance in complying with technical regulations and sanitary and phytosanitary measures applied to imported products by the mentoring countries.

❑ Third there is increasing recognition that the policy approaches adopted by developed countries in the technical level discussions on formulation of standards are greatly influenced by their industries. This has resulted in international standards in a number of product areas being developed on the basis of standards used by manufacturers and producers from developed countries.

Although the technological divide between the developed countries in the North and the developing countries of the South is gradually narrowing, there are still wide differences in the processes and production methods used in manufacturing in these two groups of countries. This also results in characteristics of products produced in developing countries, particularly of simple manufactured products, being different from similar products produced in developed countries. In the area of food products, there are often major differences between the national regulations in developing countries and those applicable in developed countries in regard to the additives and colouring ingredients that may be used, and in the permissible maximum residue levels (MRLs). National standards used also vary from country to country because of differences in climatic and environmental conditions. If these differences are to be adequately reflected in the technical work at international level on standards formulation so that the international standards adopted are not based only on the standards applied in developed countries, it is necessary to ensure that the assistance provided under the mentoring and twinning arrangements is extended to requesting countries, wherever possible, by developing countries with the necessary expertise and technical competence.

In this context it is important to note that in their joint report the consultants emphasized the need to put greater reliance on South-South cooperation in providing assistance to improve participation of developing countries in the work on formulation of international standards, as well as providing assistance in other trade-related standardization areas. In particular, they observed that 'it is vital for developing countries to learn from one another, rather than looking to developed countries for finding solutions to their problems'. This is echoed in the report of the workshop on technical assistance and special and differential treatment organized by the TBT Committee in July 2000 (for details see box 7, page 42–43) on the actions that could be taken to meet the technical assistance needs of developing countries.

Main features of the framework to be established for facilitation of mentoring and twinning arrangements

The effectiveness of the mechanism in meeting the technical assistance needs of developing countries would greatly depend on how far the framework established was conducive to and effective in facilitating bilateral or plurilateral negotiations among participating countries for mentoring and twinning arrangements. Some suggestions regarding the principles and guidelines on which the mechanism could be based are made below.

❑ The programme under the mechanism would be implemented on a pilot basis.

❑ The implementing agency would be responsible for:

- Providing facilities for exchange of information on trade-related aspects of standardization and for consultations on problems and issues of interest and concern to the participating countries through its networks;

- Assisting institutions or agencies from the participating countries, engaged in work at national level in the subject area, in building up information technology infrastructures needed for exchange of information through its networks; and

- Assisting and encouraging participating countries to enter into formal and informal mentoring and twinning arrangements on bilateral and plurilateral basis.

Participation in the programme would be open initially to a limited number of interested countries. It is recognized that the programme would be viable only if a sufficient number of countries, with the technical capacities to act as mentors and willing to provide advice and assistance, agreed to join it.

The programme would be implemented in two stages. In the first stage, emphasis would be placed on providing assistance to developing countries to improve their participation in the technical level discussions in international standard-setting organizations on formulation of standards on a selected limited number of products identified as being of export interest to those developing countries and on which work on standardization is being undertaken, or is likely to be undertaken, in one of the seven international standard-setting organizations.

In the second stage, the programme would be broadened to include the possibility of extending, through mentoring and twinning arrangements, assistance to other priority areas identified by the case studies (e.g. for the establishment of national accreditation bodies, and for practical training through the secondment of officials).

The arrangement of the programme in two stages has been suggested, firstly, to make it more manageable. Secondly and perhaps more importantly, it is felt that countries would have more interest in acting as mentors to other countries to improve their participation in standardization activities as this could enable them to build up common positions in the technical discussions and negotiations on the formulation of draft standards.

Techniques and modalities for promoting dialogue between mentors and twinning countries

The effectiveness of the programme would greatly depend on the modalities used for bringing together, and promoting dialogue and exchange of views among, countries that can provide assistance and those interested in entering into twinning arrangements with them. Box 17 contains a broad outline of the preliminary information that would be required.

When the mentoring and twinning mechanism is broadened in the second stage to cover other areas identified by the case studies, modalities would have to be pursued on the basis of the experience of the operation of the first stage, assuming that there is both interest and willingness on the part of mentor countries to broaden the scope of the arrangement to other areas and on the part of twinning countries to receive such assistance.

Box 17
Basic information needed for promoting dialogue between countries who could act as mentors and those needing assistance

Information to be obtained from mentors

❑ *The names of the organizations responsible for participation in the technical level discussions (e.g. national standard-setting body, ministry or government department) in respect of each of the products in the priority list selected for coverage under mentoring and twinning arrangements.*

❑ *Whether the concerned organizations are participating in the work at technical level on the formulation of international standards for those products.*

❑ *If so, whether the government would be willing to allow those organizations to cooperate with countries participating in the programme and interested in entering into twinning arrangements by sharing with them:*

    – *Technical and other background papers prepared by them in the subject area;*

    – *Comments or proposals for modifications to the draft standards that they have made; and*

    – *The approach they propose to adopt in future discussions at technical level on the formulation of draft standards.*

    – *Whether they would be willing to provide, if requested, advice on the possible approach that the requesting country could adopt in the technical level discussions.*

Information to be provided by countries wishing to enter into twinning arrangements with mentors

❑ *Whether they are participating in the technical level discussions on formulation of standards on any of the products listed.*

❑ *What resources they are able to devote to the work.*

❑ *Which products they would be interested in entering into mentoring and twinning arrangements for.*

Creating greater awareness among industry and trade associations of the need to take more active interest in standardization activities at national and international level

The case studies have shown that there is a general lack of awareness on the part of trade and business associations, as well as consumer associations, in most of the developing countries of the important role that international standards play in facilitating trade. This often results in their not taking an active interest in undertaking the analytical work and background research necessary for advising the national standard-setting bodies, ministries or other agencies that are responsible for participating in international standardization activities.

This situation is markedly different to that prevailing in most developed countries. In these countries, the views of industry greatly influence the attitudes and approaches taken by the national standard-setting bodies or government departments when participating in the discussions at technical level on the formulation of draft standards and on their adoption as international standards. A few developing countries where the standardization infrastructure is well developed have also now adopted effective mechanisms for soliciting the views of industry on draft international standards. Industry is also responding by devoting resources to undertaking the necessary analysis and research to ensure that national standards and methods used in production are taken into account in the approach adopted for participation in the discussions at international level.

Information packages should be developed to explain the procedures adopted for formulation and development of international standards and how the support provided by the industry and business associations, through analysis and research undertaken by them, could ensure that international standards remain responsive to their national requirements for quality and safety and ensure that adoption of these standards by trading partners does not constitute unnecessary barriers to trade. Workshops should be organized to provide guidance to participating countries on the appropriate mechanisms for consultations at national level between governments, on the one hand, and industry and business associations and consumer associations, on the other hand, on the trade-related standardization issues under discussion at national, regional and international levels.

Assistance to developing countries in meeting the requirements of technical regulations and of sanitary and phytosanitary measures applied in their export markets

Provision of practical assistance

The Agreement on TBT calls on member countries to provide technical assistance to developing countries if they are experiencing problems in complying with technical regulations and conformity assessment procedures (article 11.3). A similar obligation to extend technical assistance is imposed by the Agreement on SPS, particularly in cases where the sanitary and phytosanitary requirements result in exporting countries having to make substantial investments in order to comply with them (article 9). The case studies illustrate the assistance that is being provided, notably by the EU and the United States, in fulfilment of these provisions.

Proposals to make the obligation to provide such assistance more binding are under consideration in the WTO discussions and negotiations on strengthening the provisions relating to technical assistance in the WTO Agreements.

Consideration should be given to adopting a multilateral programme to complement the assistance that is being provided on a bilateral basis, to help on request exporting developing countries that have encountered problems in complying with technical regulations and sanitary and phytosanitary measures applied by countries to which they export.

Preparation of brochures explaining technical regulations and sanitary and phytosanitary measures applicable to certain products

In addition, it may be desirable to publish brochures explaining in simple language the sanitary and phytosanitary measures applied in selected imported markets for certain products such as fresh fruits and vegetables, fish and fish products, and meat and meat products. The case studies indicate that, in a large number of cases, the problems encountered by exporters in relation to these and other agricultural products arise from a lack of knowledge of the requirements which have to be fulfilled in order to ensure that the products will be permitted entry by the importing country. Exporters also face problems because requirements vary from one importing market to another. For instance, while some countries require prior inspection of processing plants, others do not. For certain food products, while some importing countries require approval and registration by the food control authorities, others do not.

Assistance to interested developing countries for establishing systems to alert exporters to changes in technical regulations or sanitary and phytosanitary measures

With the increasing concern about food safety and the need to protect consumer interests, the number of new technical regulations and sanitary and phytosanitary measures that are being adopted in both developed and developing countries is on the increase. These concerns are also making countries lay down, particularly in their sanitary and phytosanitary measures, standards that are higher than the international standards. As noted earlier, the Agreement on SPS permits countries to adopt sanitary and phytosanitary measures that are higher than international standards if there is a scientific justification and it is established that a higher level of protection is appropriate. The Agreement on TBT also permits standards that differ from international standards in certain defined situations.

Both the Agreements, however, impose obligations on countries adopting regulations or measures that deviate from international standards to notify the products covered by them to the WTO Secretariat if they may have a significant effect on trade. Immediately on receipt these notifications are transmitted by the WTO Secretariat to the member countries for onward transmission to industry and business associations and are posted on the WTO website. As explained previously, the purpose of the notification procedure is to provide an opportunity for interested governments to comment on the draft regulations, so that the characteristics of products produced in their countries are adequately taken into account in adopting the final regulation.

The case studies have shown that many developing countries have not been able to make adequate use of this right to comment on the draft regulations. This is because the government departments responsible for further processing such notifications simply do not circulate them to the industry and trade associations.

Although the main purpose of the notifications is to enable outside countries to comment on the drafts, they also serve the purpose of warning exporting countries that new regulations or measures are being adopted, or existing ones are being modified. Compliance with regulations often requires exporting companies to change or modify their production processes and methods of production or to change product composition by withdrawing ingredients that are not allowed to be used. Such modifications and changes take time; they also often require investment. That is why the Agreement on SPS calls on countries introducing new sanitary and phytosanitary measures 'to allow longer timeframes for compliance for products of export interest to developing countries' with a view to giving them sufficient time to take steps to meet the requirements (article 10). The Agreement on TBT calls on countries to provide differential and more favourable treatment to developing country members through the provisions of article 12 as well as through the relevant provisions of other Articles in the Agreement.

Against this background it may be desirable to consider whether exporters should be helped to prepare themselves for meeting the requirements of new technical regulations or sanitary and phytosanitary measures in countries to which they export. Some efforts in this direction have been made by WTO. It has introduced a system under which a developing country can request that notifications relating to the products it has identified as being of export interest to it are transmitted to designated persons. Such pre-selection could help countries in two ways. Firstly, it may facilitate the process of examination of draft technical regulations and sanitary and phytosanitary measures. Secondly, it also acts as an early warning system for the government and for the industry and business associations to whom the notifications are circulated of the need to prepare themselves for the new requirements.

In this context it is important to note that some of the countries that have made progress in developing viable standards infrastructures have established at the national level systems for alerting exporters when new technical regulations or sanitary and phytosanitary measures are being adopted by countries to which they export.

The enquiry point for TBT and SPS in Canada, for instance, has developed a system that automatically enters notifications received from WTO into an online database coded by subject areas, using the International Classification of Standards system. Canadian companies interested in receiving notification information select the areas of interest to them, to ensure that they receive only relevant notifications. In Brazil, the enquiry point for TBT has developed a tool called *Alerta Exportador* which enables exporters to receive daily, by e-mail and without any associated cost, information on new WTO notifications on technical regulations and conformity assessment procedures, according to a predefined profile.

There is need for a 'model tool for alerting exporters' of the changes in requirements that are likely to occur as a result of the adoption of new technical regulations or sanitary and phytosanitary measures and conformity assessment systems, by using WTO notifications.

Assistance for the establishment of accreditation bodies at national and regional level

National accreditation bodies, which are authorized to accredit testing, inspection and certification bodies after evaluating their technical competence, do not exist in most of the case study countries or are not recognized at international level. In relation to imported products for which importing countries require conformity assessments there is reluctance to accept certificates issued by laboratories, inspection bodies or certification bodies that are not accredited. This often results in the imported products having to undergo further tests and inspections on importation.

A number of countries therefore need technical assistance to establish a government-recognized professional body to accredit laboratories and other conformity assessment bodies, after evaluation and site inspections undertaken in accordance with the guidelines adopted by the relevant international organizations. For some countries, it may be desirable and appropriate to establish such bodies at a regional level, or make arrangements for accreditation of conformity assessment bodies by a foreign accreditation body.

Concluding observations

Considerable emphasis has been placed on the mechanism of 'mentoring and twinning arrangements', particularly for providing assistance to improve the participation of developing countries in the work at technical level in international standardization activities. The role of the implementing agency in work in this area would therefore be confined to providing a forum for dialogue and exchange of information for countries that as mentors could provide technical assistance and those interested in entering twinning arrangements with them in order to obtain such assistance and advice. The primary responsibility for providing assistance would belong to a few countries that would be offering to act as mentors.

The extent to which the mechanism of mentoring and twinning arrangements would be effective in meeting the needs of developing countries for technical assistance to improve participation in international standardization activities and in other areas identified in this publication, would depend in the main on two factors.

First, is the existence of political will on the part of the governments of countries having technical capacities to provide assistance directly to countries needing such assistance by entering with them mentoring and twinning arrangements. In this context, it is important to keep in mind that in some of these countries national standard-setting and other bodies engaged in standardization work have a degree of autonomy.

The second related factor is the availability of financial resources to cover the cost of the technical assistance provided. Countries would be more willing to act as mentors if they were assured that adequate funds from multilateral institutions or from donor countries would be available over a reasonably long period of time to meet the costs and fees related to the provision of such assistance.

Extracts from general comments about technical assistance made by the six consultants based on the twelve case studies

Some observations concerning implementation of WTO obligations in relation to the development and use of international standards

General observations and study limitations

There were three teams of consultants, each comprising an SPS expert and a TBT expert. Each team visited two of the case study countries for a period of between one and two weeks. A significant part of this time was taken up by the collection of background information on relevant trade patterns, administrative arrangements and responsibilities for SPS and TBT measures, participation in international standard-setting organizations, key policy initiatives and so forth. The relevant government agencies and private sector organizations cooperated actively to support the work of the consultants. Even so, the teams could not be expected in the time available to develop a detailed understanding of every aspect of each country's SPS or TBT regime.

As anticipated, the case studies revealed substantial differences between the countries examined in terms of most of the parameters under consideration. Although there are risks in attempting to draw generalizations from the studies, some common themes emerged. They are reflected in the discussion that follows.

Observations concerning implementation of SPS obligations

The difficulties for developing countries are in three broad areas:

❏ Developing countries' human and financial resources are extremely limited by comparison with the resources required to meet their obligations and to take full advantage of their rights under the Agreement on SPS. These constraints also limit the ability of developing countries to participate effectively in the setting of international standards. Consequently, questions are raised about the extent to which international standards take proper account of the needs and special circumstances of developing countries. This issue is particularly salient in view of the status given to international standards within the Agreements on TBT and, in particular, SPS.

❏ There is a propensity for some developed countries to set conditions for access above prevailing international standards, and to vary their requirements over time, in such a way as to increase the difficulty for developing countries of meeting market access conditions. Some developed countries may impose conditions on imports from developing countries that are more stringent than those applied domestically, e.g. if greater food safety risks are associated with imports.

❑ Administrative structures and legislative systems in developing countries can impose further constraints on their ability to comply with SPS and TBT measures in developed countries.

Predictably the extent to which the case study countries apply international standards as the basis of their sanitary and phytosanitary measures varies widely, reflecting among other things the level and composition of economic activity and the pattern of trade. For example Mauritius, which is a substantial importer of food and has a well-developed food control system, uses all relevant Codex standards as the basis for its own standards. On the other hand Namibia, also a substantial food importer, does not appear to have a well-developed food control system and still relies on South Africa's standards.

Overall, Codex standards appear to be well accepted and are widely used to the extent that national standards are in place; there was little evidence of the use of regional standards or the development and adoption of national standards significantly different from a corresponding international norm. Similarly, OIE standards and codes are typically the basis of national standards for animal health, although in several of the case study countries it is very difficult to maintain effective animal health regimes. The situation with respect to plant health standards is somewhat different. To date, the norms established by IPPC have tended to relate to definitions and concepts, methods and methodology, and administrative procedures rather than to control of specific pest risks. In part, this reflects the fact that IPPC did not perform the role of establishing international standards until the mid-1990s and is still in the early stages of its standard-setting programme. However, it also reflects the fact that pest and disease problems differ markedly between countries.

One important international phytosanitary measure, especially from the perspective of obligations under the Agreement on SPS, is that dealing with appropriate pest risk analysis. Consultations within the case study countries suggested that this is an area where developing countries have particular difficulty in following the international norm. Namibia and Uganda were not signatories to the 1979 International Plant Protection Convention, although they are expected to sign the latest Convention in the near future.

Concerning participation in the relevant international standard-setting organizations, most of the case study countries (with the exception of Malaysia) found it difficult to engage in an effective way at the technical level where standards are developed. Typically, countries are able to be represented when the plenary bodies meet, especially in OIE, which provides some assistance to meet the subsistence costs of delegates. However, the ability of five of the six case study countries to be influential in these organizations is limited by a number of factors including the lack of depth in their scientific resources, financial resource limitations and the difficulty of maintaining continuity of participation. In turn, their knowledge and experience of the procedures of these organizations tends to be limited and, as a consequence, their influence is limited even when they are able to attend meetings.

In contrast, the case studies showed that countries do maintain effective sanitary and phytosanitary regimes in relation to some of the most immediate and important health risks – for example the exclusion of sugar cane pests from Mauritius and Namibia's continuing freedom from foot and mouth disease – while not being able to exert effective control over other risks – for example the uncontrolled import of foods (other than meat) into Namibia, and the movement of animals, plants and their products across the borders of Kenya and Uganda. Furthermore, there is evidence that, when SPS or TBT requirements threaten their economic interests, the case study countries are willing and able to take action. In Jamaica, for example, the Government has taken decisive action to address problems with exports to the United States relating to pesticide residues in callaloo and yam, and insect pests on hot peppers. The Jamaican Government has entered into bilateral negotiations with United States authorities and established national task forces to identify and implement the required action at national level.

All of the case study countries encounter sanitary or phytosanitary barriers to their exports. Although their authorities and the producer representative bodies note that it may be difficult to conform with the international norms when they are applied by developed importing countries (as sanctioned by the Agreement on SPS), the greater problem for them is often the imposition by importing countries of requirements that are stricter than the relevant international norm – as in the case of EU requirements concerning meat-processing plants. In very few cases had these concerns been raised through the SPS Committee. Rather, to the extent that any action had been taken, this had been pursued on a bilateral basis with the country concerned. Although there were examples of this strategy being successful, there was a general frustration about the time taken for countries to respond and/or attend to the issue and (if pertinent) for the offending measures to be revised.

In general, the basic institutions required by the Agreement on SPS to meet transparency obligations are in place in the case study countries, with one or two exceptions. Systems for dissemination of information from the SPS enquiry and notification points to stakeholders within the public and private sectors in the case study countries are, however, often ineffective. Likewise, administrative structures that aim to identify the problems faced by exporters are generally lacking and/or are overly bureaucratic. Attendance at meetings of the SPS Committee is sporadic for most of these countries.

Observations concerning implementation of TBT obligations

It became evident that not all developing countries are able to comply with TBT obligations.

Participation in the preparation of international standards by international standard-setting organizations is infrequent. The most common constraint seemed to be insufficient funds, and the unavailability of experts to represent the country. Since most of the countries are net importers and offer few manufactured products for export, relevance of the standards under discussion to the country's needs for export was also mentioned. In contrast, however, meetings at higher level where decisions are made on policy matters are well attended and pose few problems.

The countries that were included in this study appear to have varying degrees of success with the structures that were established to comply with the requirements of the Agreement on TBT; some were poorly organized and in some areas they may not have been functioning at all. The national enquiry points may, for example, have been established, but they were not fully functional yet. Personnel, training and equipment constraints were the main reasons provided.

In most countries it was observed that industry (including small and medium-sized enterprises), commerce, and some government circles were generally not well informed or aware of the Agreement on TBT and its implications. Information was not disseminated successfully, mostly as a result of some of the structures referred to previously not being fully functional at this stage.

Conformity assessment structures and procedures were often limited by lack of equipment, or poorly maintained equipment. Laboratory accreditation was not regarded as a high priority in some of the countries. Laboratory equipment needs constant maintenance, repair and calibration. In the countries visited no such facilities are available and equipment has to be shipped overseas at great expense for servicing. This is also one of the reasons provided for the inability of laboratories to achieve accreditation.

It was observed that various aid providing organizations donated equipment or provided training, but this was carried out in an uncoordinated manner, which often resulted in equipment not being utilized, or in services being duplicated.

General considerations concerning needs for technical assistance in this area

While technical assistance requirements are frequently highly country-specific, the case studies did identify a number of general issues concerning needs for technical assistance.

Technical assistance needs are specific to circumstances of each country and cannot be defined simply as the gap between developed and developing countries

Developing countries have reached various stages in implementing the Agreements on SPS and TBT. Some countries have a very low level of development in terms of structures for handling SPS and TBT issues for their exports; some countries have rudimentary structures that do not operate very well; while other countries have structures that work, in some cases as well as in developed countries, but need additional capacity in a few specific areas.

Not all developing countries are at the same level of industrial development, and needs for technical assistance vary accordingly. It is important therefore that specific needs of each country be identified, evaluated and quantified in terms of resources needed, relevance to the resolution of the problems, and cost of technical assistance. Furthermore, there are clear differences between the needs and priorities of food-importing and food-exporting countries.

In a number of cases the problems with SPS and TBT measures faced by developing countries relate to products that are insignificant in terms of world trade. Consequently, it is unlikely that international standards will be developed, at least in the near future, to establish norms that can be applied to trade. Exports of traditional vegetables from Jamaica (for example callaloo, yam and ackee) provide a good example.

Technical assistance should not duplicate capacities existing in developed countries but should aim at solving a defined problem by developing capacities that are tailor-made to the needs of the country depending on the type of the problem at hand and the export products of importance to the country. In so doing, consideration may be given to including products that a country has been trying to export but has been unable to because of SPS or TBT requirements of importing countries.

In many cases, the task of undertaking the preliminary identification of needs has to be done by the developing countries themselves.

The amount of technical assistance available in this field is likely to be greatly exceeded by the aggregate value of worthwhile projects

Developing an infrastructure for handling SPS and TBT issues requires substantial resources. Developing countries entered the new era of the SPS and TBT regimes in 1995 with a substantial deficit in terms of their technical capacity in relation to standards and conformity assessment compared to developed countries. (Even for developed countries it is difficult to fully implement all of the obligations under the two Agreements, especially in areas such as risk assessment as the basis of sanitary and phytosanitary measures.) Moreover, technical requirements of importing countries tend over time to become more demanding and more complex, putting commensurately greater demands on the conformity assessment and other capacities of exporting countries. Improvements in knowledge and analytical techniques that are available in developed countries give rise to new perceptions of risk and an expectation that the same knowledge and techniques will be employed in exporting countries. For these and other reasons the level of technical assistance needed is likely to exceed the level of resources available. In one of the countries visited, technical assistance amounting to US$ 6 million had been agreed upon by donors, but eventually only US$ 3 million was provided. Furthermore, the approval and eventual delivery of technical assistance can take a considerable period of time. In some of the case study countries this had caused frustration and a view that their problems were not being taken seriously.

Available technical assistance should be targeted to the most cost effective uses and waste should be reduced or avoided

Technical assistance should be targeted to areas where there is the greatest need and the return from investment of resources will be highest. An appropriate balance will need to be maintained between meeting immediate needs and longer-term capacity building. Existing structures should be carefully evaluated before technical assistance is given for the development of new ones; strengthening existing structures may be the most cost-effective solution. Consideration must be given to the mandate of the existing structure and whether this mandate could be legally expanded.

To avoid waste, existing and previous technical assistance offered should be made known and evaluated before new assistance is given. Thus, new technical assistance should aim as complementing ongoing or previous assistance.

Apparent fragmentation of previous technical assistance should be addressed

It is apparent that in many cases previous technical assistance given to some developing countries, in the areas of SPS and TBT in particular, was fragmented. This has led to gaps in the development of competencies. In some cases too little assistance was given in comparison to the identified need. In other cases, reasonable assistance was given by two or more agencies at different times to address the same issues, thus duplicating efforts without any additional benefits to the country concerned.

There is thus a need for an integrated approach and coordination in the provision of technical assistance to avoid duplication. The SPS Committee* has an important role to play in this respect. Indeed, it has recently made efforts to

---

*   This applies to the TBT Committee as well.

gather information on technical assistance that has been provided and encouraged the use of a standard typology to enable more effective management of technical assistance. Furthermore, Members have been encouraged to put forward their technical assistance needs at meetings of the SPS Committee. The response to such requests is then highlighted and can be discussed.

Planning and prioritizing technical assistance

The case studies collectively indicate that there are differences in the extent of the development assistance needs between the countries visited. Nevertheless, collectively, and particularly having regard to those needs being common to many developing countries, very substantial long-term technical assistance requirements exist. Without targeted technical assistance based on a sound strategy, and in-country commitment to support the efforts made, it is highly unlikely that developing countries will be able to extract benefits from the existence of the Agreements on TBT and SPS.

Much of the assistance provided by development assistance agencies over many years in areas that underpin SPS activities, such as animal and plant health, has been based on a fragmented approach and as such has not been sustainable. At times, duplicative funding of projects with quite similar goals has occurred. For example, project funding provided by German Technical Cooperation through the SADC Secretariat for the SADC SPS/Food Safety Conference of November 2000 facilitated the preparation of country papers that covered issues similar to those of this study, at least in respect of Namibia and Mauritius. Furthermore, USAID is currently funding a project that aims to enhance the SPS capacity of SADC member countries. Additionally, the World Bank has flagged the intention of funding a not dissimilar study involving several of the African countries covered by this study.[*]

There are significant potential savings to be made from improved coordination arrangements in respect of SPS and TBT related development assistance:

❑ Development assistance in the areas covered by this study is necessarily technical in nature. However, many development assistance agencies do not have the technical capacity to appropriately evaluate proposals for assistance. Additionally there is no focal point where development assistance agencies can obtain advice.

❑ The effectiveness of development assistance related to training has not been maximized. As an example, in the Pacific and in African countries a range of agencies has provided considerable training relating to pest risk analysis. However, for many countries providing this training can be compared to training a carpenter but that carpenter then having no tools (equipment) or timber (resources) to actually work with.

❑ There appears to have been an unwillingness of development assistance agencies to ensure that technical assistance in the form of capacity-building projects is matched by complementary effort on the part of the recipient country; for example, key coordinating ministries such as Finance/Treasury and the Public Service Commission are not 'locked in' during the project design phase. Accordingly there is little commitment to provide the ongoing support that is essential for sustainable progress in capacity-building projects.

---

[*]   Results are available in *Standards & Global Trade: A Voice for Africa*, published by the World Bank in 2003.

❑ Very rarely is a capacity-building project terminated when it becomes obvious that sustainable gains will not be realized.

❑ Some countries appear to be more concerned to maximize development assistance rather than the effectiveness of that assistance.

One of the most significant problems has been the lack of effective prioritizing and planning mechanisms within developing countries. As a result, technical assistance has not been directed towards the areas of greatest need. Technical assistance priorities need to be linked to specific (soundly based) trade initiatives of the private sector. A simple planning framework is needed that builds in national priorities and operates on the basis of performance-reporting linked to targets and milestones for both the country and the organization responsible for project implementation.

In many cases technical assistance has been built on to an in-country base that cannot sustain the improvements planned. For example sophisticated laboratory equipment may have been provided even though the recipient country does not have the means or is unwilling to commit to provide the skilled human resources to operate it, essential maintenance, consumables and so forth. Indeed, it is possible for excess capacity to be developed that is beyond the needs of developing country exporters. Not only does this waste scarce technical assistance, but it can tie developing countries into longer-term resource demands to maintain this capacity. This underlines the need for technical assistance to be 'appropriate' and problem-focused.

In the areas of SPS and TBT a sound approach given the technical nature of the assistance will involve a focal point where:

❑ Advice can be obtained on the SPS/TBT needs of particular countries having regard to the assessed or known stage of development of the country.

❑ Advice can be obtained in relation to complementary work in that country or region (perhaps by a regional organization) which may influence the specific nature of technical assistance.

❑ The work programmes of international organizations such as CAC and OIE, and regional plant protection organizations are considered in relation to the planned development assistance.

It may be the case that at times technical assistance should be directed towards building regional capacity as distinct from national capacity. For example:

❑ Laboratory capacity capable of non-routine (i.e. reference) testing may be better provided at a regional laboratory. It may not, however, be practical when it comes to routine testing where results may be required within a relatively short space of time. A case in point is Namibia, where exporters commented about the time taken to get results for metal residues in fish from the testing facility used in South Africa. The exporters felt that a local facility was needed to enable results to be obtained more quickly.

❑ Record-keeping activities including the ability to access previous scientific studies and pest and disease information could be managed by a regional organization. With the countries of Africa having many land borders, over time pest and diseases present in one country tend also to be present in neighbouring countries. Consequently scientific studies relevant to a specific pest or disease in one country are likely to be of interest to other countries in the region.

❑ If developing countries want to challenge specific measures applied over and above international standards by some importing countries, a regional approach may be much more effective than effort by an individual exporting country.

Examples of appropriate technical assistance and ideas for further research

Specific product technical assistance

Specific product technical assistance is detailed in the individual country reports of the consultants. There is a need to target some at least of the technical assistance towards facilitating the achievement of specific export objectives via minimization or elimination of technical barriers to trade in a timely way. What is needed for each country is the development of an export market access strategy in which particular sanitary and phytosanitary barriers are targeted on the basis of industry views about the highest priorities. This would be followed by an assessment of what barriers are actually capable of being overcome; then each high priority barrier would be tackled by means of a progressive approach involving appropriate technical development (for example compilation of a pest risk assessment or establishing an effective treatment regime) and then step-by-step representations on a bilateral basis leading on to WTO dispute settlement if necessary.

From the perspective of donors the issue is then how to support this integrated approach by injecting assistance where it is most needed in a targeted way over time. A typical situation might be where a country has domestic and perhaps regional markets for a certain product and is looking to access the more lucrative EU, United States or Japanese markets. If there is the prospect of building up a profitable export trade into these markets for the product then what are the technical barriers and what needs to be done to overcome them? Donors can assist in a programmed way that complements national industry and government efforts.

Capacity-building technical assistance

Long-term technical assistance is needed in the form of regional investment in scientific and technical infrastructure, including laboratory facilities, research facilities, attachments for staff and access to scientific and technical journals and books. Because this is envisaged as long-term assistance it is vitally important that these efforts be coordinated and carefully attuned to developing country priorities and their capacity to sustain improvements. Effort should be concentrated on tradeable products that have the best chance of making a significant contribution to national economic welfare over the longer term.

The development and maintenance of an SPS capacity database

This could involve developing a questionnaire for completion by developing countries. This questionnaire would be designed to be completed by the country, as distinct from a visiting consultant, with countries being advised that their response will be indicative of their interest. Certain initiatives have been taken to develop a questionnaire for assessing SPS capacity. The Inter-American Institute for Cooperation on Agriculture (IICA) has developed a measurement instrument and applied it to assess SPS capacity among its 34 member countries. The instrument is now being refined in the light of these preliminary results. The IPPC Secretariat has collaborated in the development of a questionnaire for self-assessment of plant protection capacity. This has been successfully applied to a number of developing countries. Furthermore, the SPS Secretariat has been developing a generic questionnaire for assessing SPS capacity that will be distributed among members.

Building this capacity may also involve maintaining a central database, updated on the basis of annual country-supplied information, which provides a picture of the current capacity of the country and SPS/TBT development assistance received during the year. This information should be supplemented by an assessment of the sustainability of development assistance provided so far. That is, has the country been able to maintain and build on previous development assistance efforts?

Following development of this questionnaire, consideration should be given to identifying developing countries that have the capacity to help other developing countries in the region.

Developing a model framework to assist countries in determining their SPS/TBT development assistance priorities

In addition to helping to prioritize access requests, which is discussed above, there is a need to provide advice on how administrative structures in developing countries can be best organized so as to maximize their ability to extract benefits from the Agreement on SPS, noting that functions such as research and extension must be closely integrated into their market access efforts in the SPS area where resources are limited. Key issues include the need to avoid over-fragmentation of governmental responsibilities for SPS and TBT measures, as well as trade issues more generally, for administrative structures to be transparent, and for all stakeholders to be actively involved in the development of national strategies to address SPS and TBT issues. The case studies provide many examples of both good and bad practice in this respect that provide valuable insights for developing countries more generally. Indeed, it is vital for developing countries to learn from one another, rather than looking to developed countries (which do not face the same resource constraints) for possible solutions to their problems.

The importance of tertiary education

There is a need to better inform tertiary education institutions in developing countries of SPS and TBT trade-related aspects of post-graduate studies relating to trade and food and agricultural sciences. In many developing countries agriculture and food, and the related sciences, are not seen as attractive careers. Placing more emphasis on the direct relationship between international trade and the agricultural and food sciences in the context of the Agreements on SPS and TBT will make post-graduate study in these areas both more relevant and more attractive to potential students.

Establishment and strengthening of WTO TBT/SPS notification and enquiry points

Technical assistance is required to facilitate improvement of computing and communications infrastructure, including access to e-mail and the Internet, to enable developing countries to participate in electronic forums for discussion and use electronic modes of voting, remote meetings and access to information sources relevant to international standard-setting. Technical assistance should also be provided to adapt for this use facilities already available in commercial software packages (for example MSN Net Meeting), all this being another way to get around the request for funds to attend meetings, which can only be supported in the short term. Technical assistance in this area should cover both provision of equipment and training of personnel.

In relation to web-based material, an enormous amount of information, both raw and processed for easy digestion, can be obtained at very little cost from the websites of international organizations. Even if Internet access in developing countries is expensive by comparison with developed countries, the absolute costs of access are still very low for all.

In the course of their investigations the consultants saw little evidence that this resource was being even partially exploited. At the same time it was apparent that the extent of knowledge among most stakeholders about the structure, functions and programmes of the ISSOs and WTO is quite low. It may be that the reason the resource is under-utilized is that there is a lack of interest, which in turn reflects a sense on the part of stakeholders that the activities in question are not relevant to them. If this is the case, there is some merit in directing technical assistance towards trying to make people appreciate what is readily already available to them.

Encouraging the provision of tangible technical assistance under article 9 of the Agreement on SPS*

The countries visited have received some technical assistance under article 9; typically this assistance has involved capacity building through training workshops. However, having regard to the scarcity of human and financial resources in developing countries, if they are to be assisted to extract real benefits from the SPS provisions, for example by increasing their exports of agricultural products, specific tangible technical assistance is required. In the case of plant products this might take the form of bringing together the necessary information that will support a pest risk analysis request. It will be important that technical assistance of this type reflects a sound prioritizing approach for the requesting country. Also important will be a long-term commitment from the country to provide the resources needed to support the continued export of the particular product. A problem worthy of particular consideration is how to establish and then maintain over time a proper articulation of technical assistance with national expenditure programmes targeted towards SPS and TBT issues.

As discussed above, the SPS Committee has a valuable role to play in monitoring provision of technical assistance to ensure that assistance is well targeted and to minimize the risk of repetition or overlap of different initiatives. There is evidence that the SPS Committee is beginning to perform this function, although it is clear that many donors are reluctant to relinquish any control over the technical assistance they provide.

Reviewing the modus operandi of international organizations

At present the standard-setting functions of international organizations to a large extent represent the views of developed countries, as it is those countries that have the capacity to make a substantive scientific input. It is difficult to envisage a situation where all developing countries have the scientific capacity to effectively influence standards development within these organizations. Yet it is important that the views of developing countries are considered, as otherwise the development of standards will mean that these countries fall further and further behind in terms of their capacity to extract trade benefits from international standards.

There is a need for international standard-setting organizations to review their administrative structures and procedures to minimize potential constraints to developing country participation. Key issues might include the location of

---

*   Also applicable under Article 11 of the TBT Agreement.

meetings, provisions for voting by post or through e-mail, and procedures for allocating administrative responsibilities. It is evident that many of the major international standard-setting organizations are taking these issues seriously and attempting to find effective ways through which developing country participation might be enhanced. However, it is evident that much more still needs to be done.

The establishment of specific regional technical capacity, to service a group of developing countries, could be considered. This capacity would provide a focus for the views of the developing countries serviced and would provide mentoring capacity for the development of in-country capacity.

Strengthening regional capacity, including the establishment of regional laboratories or regional laboratory maintenance centres

Strengthening regional capacity is likely to be beneficial in a number of areas:

❑ Laboratory facilities. There is a need for technical assistance in the development of regional laboratories and/or regional centres for the maintenance of laboratory equipment. This is in recognition of the fact that to counteract technical barriers imposed on exports of the developing countries it is often necessary to test these products, which of course requires that the equipment be functioning properly and the laboratory assessed as satisfying the related conformity assessment standards. It is suggested that this would be more likely to be sustainable as a regional project rather than a national one. It should be pointed out that it is envisaged that this technical assistance may have to take the form of persuading the manufacturers of analytical equipment to assist in the setting up of joint repair facilities in the region (rather than having the equipment sent back to their individual facilities for repair or servicing).

In relation to laboratory capacity, tissue culture may also represent an area where regional capacity is likely to be much more sustainable than specific national capacity. However, it is important to recognize that there may be practical difficulties in relation to regional laboratories used for conformity assessment, as the time taken to transport samples to a laboratory may cause difficulties for the acceptability of results. As a general principle, regional laboratories are likely to be more useful in research situations than in conformity assessment.

❑ Technical advice. Providing regional capacity able to coordinate and deliver input for countries of a region is likely to increase the extent of the input of developing countries to standards development. Building national capacity in these areas is not likely to be cost-effective or sustainable in the medium to long term.

Options for pursuing this strengthening of regional capacity include strengthening organizations such as SADC; ideally the strengthening would occur in an organization that is able to service all countries of a region. Alternatively, appropriately resourced offices of the key international organizations could be established in the regions. This could be done more cost-effectively by siting the office within a national standard-setting body and stocking it with equipment that would facilitate access to the headquarters of the organization. Careful consideration would need to be given to the type and number of personnel proposed so as to ensure the cost-effective use of the expertise.

Mentoring and training of trainers in WTO SPS/TBT issues as well as technical areas such as HACCP and pest risk analysis

Technical assistance is needed to make the population, particularly including stakeholders, of the developing countries more aware of the importance and relevance of the WTO rules on technical barriers to trade (SPS or TBT) so as to encourage the ready development of national positions on issues sent to the country for comment. From our observations the level of understanding is somewhat superficial amongst important stakeholders when in reality the WTO Agreements are extremely important to the economic prospects of many developing countries and well-informed national opinion is the necessary basis for national commitment to use WTO rights intelligently and effectively. To raise the level of understanding will require careful consideration of the most cost-effective approaches; the optimal mix will probably include training of several key people in other countries or at WTO, national training courses for opinion leaders and policy-makers, printed material for distribution to identified target groups such as growers, and so forth. Training is also required to help industry to become HACCP compliant, so that market access can be facilitated where HACCP requirements exist. It is considered important that these should be train-the-trainer type programmes, so that they may eventually replace the dependence on external trainers and become sustainable over time. Training should be substantially oriented towards private sector participants.

It is possible to develop mentoring arrangements and, if the country has reasonable Internet capacity, to largely operate them via e-mail. The establishment of regional mentoring arrangements in developed countries is likely to enhance knowledge of the needs and capacity of developing countries to build on development assistance efforts. The Pacific Pest Net is an example of a regionally based e-mail mentoring service that assists small Pacific countries with specific pest and disease information and advice.

Increasing practical transparency under the Agreements on SPS and TBT

Increasing the capacity of developing countries is important, but some developed countries constantly impose high and complex requirements, so in effect the developing countries can never catch up.

Given the impact of the development of 'new issue' standards on developing countries, it will be important to create a mechanism to conduct a rigorous assessment of the impact of these standards on developing countries.

A number of the developing countries visited expressed concern that they were asked to implement standards from certain developed countries that were higher than international standards. Additionally they did not believe that the particular standards were being enforced on a national basis to the degree that they were enforced for countries wishing to access the particular market.

It would be appropriate to consider the development of a mechanism that logically attaches to the transparency provisions of the Agreements on SPS and TBT. This mechanism would allow for an independent assessment (when requested) of whether a developed country's enforcement activities are equivalent to those being required of exporting countries.

Considering a wider application of the provisions relating to the consistency of sanitary and phytosanitary measures in developed countries where higher than international standards are regularly used is also likely to be of benefit to developing countries.

The establishment of a trust fund

The establishment of a trust fund directed towards providing specific technical assistance to developing countries could be usefully researched. In part this may be used to overcome the (political) reluctance of some countries towards providing technical assistance of a nature that would lead to increased imports from developing countries. Both CAC and IPPC have explored the possibility of establishing a trust fund aimed at enhancing participation in their standard-setting procedures. Furthermore, FAO has established trust funds in some areas aimed at the provision of technical assistance relating to agricultural and food products.

Dispute settlement mechanisms

The WTO Dispute Settlement Understanding adopted as one of the outcomes of the Uruguay Round appears to be quite effective. All of the significant complaints about SPS issues that have entered the formal procedures have been resolved in favour of the complaining Member(s). There have been no formal disputes heard by a dispute settlement panel on a TBT issue.

However, it is very expensive for both complaining and defending parties to have a dispute resolved through the WTO dispute settlement mechanism unless the matter is settled at an early stage. Proceedings involving panels are largely beyond the capacity of small developing countries to support individually. A review of this mechanism in terms of the ability of developing countries to utilize the provisions effectively will assist developing countries, a number of which hold concerns in relation to SPS standards and barriers but have no capacity to effectively pursue their concerns.

The recent establishment of the Advisory Centre for WTO Law is a very positive initiative that addresses, in part, the problems that developing countries face in pursuing a complaint through the WTO's dispute settlement mechanism. However, it is imperative that developing countries demonstrate the value of this initiative by becoming members.

Regional workshops

A logical first step would be to hold a series of regional workshops to discuss how best to develop the themes presented by this study. These workshops for SPS issues* should be attended by:

❑ ITC, WTO SPS Secretariat, OIE, IPPC and CAC representatives.

❑ Key development assistance agencies active in the region, including FAO.

❑ Government officials from countries in each region.

❑ Key stakeholders from countries in the region representing agricultural producers, food industry, exporters, consumers and other elements of civil society.

At these workshops, developing countries should be encouraged to share experiences and learn from the initiatives taken by comparable countries in seeking solutions to their problems. This final point is a key conclusion of the study – in developing effective strategies to address their SPS and TBT issues, developing countries can learn better from other developing countries that face similar conditions and resource constraints than from developed countries.

---

* Similar workshops can be organized for TBT issues and should be attended by representatives of the relevant bodies/structures.

Agreement on Technical Barriers to Trade

Members,

Having regard to the Uruguay Round of Multilateral Trade Negotiations;

Desiring to further the objectives of GATT 1994;

Recognizing the important contribution that international standards and conformity assessment systems can make in this regard by improving efficiency of production and facilitating the conduct of international trade;

Desiring therefore to encourage the development of such international standards and conformity assessment systems;

Desiring however to ensure that technical regulations and standards, including packaging, marking and labelling requirements, and procedures for assessment of conformity with technical regulations and standards do not create unnecessary obstacles to international trade;

Recognizing that no country should be prevented from taking measures necessary to ensure the quality of its exports, or for the protection of human, animal or plant life or health, of the environment, or for the prevention of deceptive practices, at the levels it considers appropriate, subject to the requirement that they are not applied in a manner which would constitute a means of arbitrary or unjustifiable discrimination between countries where the same conditions prevail or a disguised restriction on international trade, and are otherwise in accordance with the provisions of this Agreement;

Recognizing that no country should be prevented from taking measures necessary for the protection of its essential security interest;

Recognizing the contribution which international standardization can make to the transfer of technology from developed to developing countries;

Recognizing that developing countries may encounter special difficulties in the formulation and application of technical regulations and standards and procedures for assessment of conformity with technical regulations and standards, and desiring to assist them in their endeavours in this regard;

Hereby *agree* as follows:

Article 1

General Provisions

1.1   General terms for standardization and procedures for assessment of conformity shall normally have the meaning given to them by definitions adopted within the United Nations system and by international standardizing bodies taking into account their context and in the light of the object and purpose of this Agreement.

1.2   However, for the purposes of this Agreement the meaning of the terms given in Annex 1 applies.

1.3   All products, including industrial and agricultural products, shall be subject to the provisions of this Agreement.

1.4   Purchasing specifications prepared by governmental bodies for production or consumption requirements of governmental bodies are not subject to the provisions of this Agreement but are addressed in the Agreement on Government Procurement, according to its coverage.

1.5   The provisions of this Agreement do not apply to sanitary and phytosanitary measures as defined in Annex A of the Agreement on the Application of Sanitary and Phytosanitary Measures.

1.6   All references in this Agreement to technical regulations, standards and conformity assessment procedures shall be construed to include any amendments thereto and any additions to the rules or the product coverage thereof, except amendments and additions of an insignificant nature.

TECHNICAL REGULATIONS AND STANDARDS

Article 2

Preparation, Adoption and Application of Technical Regulations by Central Government Bodies

With respect to their central government bodies:

2.1   Members shall ensure that in respect of technical regulations, products imported from the territory of any Member shall be accorded treatment no less favourable than that accorded to like products of national origin and to like products originating in any other country.

2.2   Members shall ensure that technical regulations are not prepared, adopted or applied with a view to or with the effect of creating unnecessary obstacles to international trade. For this purpose, technical regulations shall not be more trade-restrictive than necessary to fulfil a legitimate objective, taking account of the risks non-fulfilment would create. Such legitimate objectives are, *inter alia:* national security requirements; the prevention of deceptive practices; protection of human health or safety, animal or plant life or health, or the environment. In assessing such risks, relevant elements of consideration are, *inter alia:* available scientific and technical information, related processing technology or intended end-uses of products.

2.3   Technical regulations shall not be maintained if the circumstances or objectives giving rise to their adoption no longer exist or if the changed circumstances or objectives can be addressed in a less trade-restrictive manner.

2.4   Where technical regulations are required and relevant international standards exist or their completion is imminent, Members shall use them, or the relevant parts of them, as a basis for their technical regulations except when such international standards or relevant parts would be an ineffective or inappropriate means for the fulfilment of the legitimate objectives pursued, for instance because of fundamental climatic or geographical factors or fundamental technological problems.

2.5   A Member preparing, adopting or applying a technical regulation which may have a significant effect on trade of other Members shall, upon the request of another Member, explain the justification for that technical regulation in terms of the provisions of paragraphs 2 to 4. Whenever a technical regulation is prepared, adopted or applied for one of the legitimate objectives explicitly mentioned in paragraph 2, and is in accordance with relevant international standards, it shall be rebuttably presumed not to create an unnecessary obstacle to international trade.

2.6   With a view to harmonizing technical regulations on as wide a basis as possible, Members shall play a full part, within the limits of their resources, in the preparation by appropriate international standardizing bodies of international standards for products for which they either have adopted, or expect to adopt, technical regulations.

2.7   Members shall give positive consideration to accepting as equivalent technical regulations of other Members, even if these regulations differ from their own, provided they are satisfied that these regulations adequately fulfil the objectives of their own regulations.

2.8   Wherever appropriate, Members shall specify technical regulations based on product requirements in terms of performance rather than design or descriptive characteristics.

2.9   Whenever a relevant international standard does not exist or the technical content of a proposed technical regulation is not in accordance with the technical content of relevant international standards, and if the technical regulation may have a significant effect on trade of other Members, Members shall:

> 2.9.1   publish a notice in a publication at an early appropriate stage, in such a manner as to enable interested parties in other Members to become acquainted with it, that they propose to introduce a particular technical regulation;
>
> 2.9.2   notify other Members through the Secretariat of the products to be covered by the proposed technical regulation, together with a brief indication of its objective and rationale. Such notifications shall take place at an early appropriate stage, when amendments can still be introduced and comments taken into account;
>
> 2.9.3   upon request, provide to other Members particulars or copies of the proposed technical regulation and, whenever possible, identify the parts which in substance deviate from relevant international standards;
>
> 2.9.4   without discrimination, allow reasonable time for other Members to make comments in writing, discuss these comments upon request, and take these written comments and the results of these discussions into account.

2.10   Subject to the provisions in the lead-in to paragraph 9, where urgent problems of safety, health, environmental protection or national security arise or threaten to arise for a Member, that Member may omit such of the steps enumerated in paragraph 9 as it finds necessary, provided that the Member, upon adoption of a technical regulation, shall:

> 2.10.1 notify immediately other Members through the Secretariat of the particular technical regulation and the products covered, with a brief indication of the objective and the rationale of the technical regulation, including the nature of the urgent problems;
>
> 2.10.2 upon request, provide other Members with copies of the technical regulation;
>
> 2.10.3 without discrimination, allow other Members to present their comments in writing, discuss these comments upon request, and take these written comments and the results of these discussions into account.

2.11   Members shall ensure that all technical regulations which have been adopted are published promptly or otherwise made available in such a manner as to enable interested parties in other Members to become acquainted with them.

2.12   Except in those urgent circumstances referred to in paragraph 10, Members shall allow a reasonable interval between the publication of technical regulations and their entry into force in order to allow time for producers in exporting Members, and particularly in developing country Members, to adapt their products or methods of production to the requirements of the importing Member.

Article 3

Preparation, Adoption and Application of Technical Regulations by Local Government Bodies and Non-Governmental Bodies

With respect to their local government and non-governmental bodies within their territories:

3.1   Members shall take such reasonable measures as may be available to them to ensure compliance by such bodies with the provisions of Article 2, with the exception of the obligation to notify as referred to in paragraphs 9.2 and 10.1 of Article 2.

3.2   Members shall ensure that the technical regulations of local governments on the level directly below that of the central government in Members are notified in accordance with the provisions of paragraphs 9.2 and 10.1 of Article 2, noting that notification shall not be required for technical regulations the technical content of which is substantially the same as that of previously notified technical regulations of central government bodies of the Member concerned.

3.3   Members may require contact with other Members, including the notifications, provision of information, comments and discussions referred to in paragraphs 9 and 10 of Article 2, to take place through the central government.

3.4   Members shall not take measures which require or encourage local government bodies or non-governmental bodies within their territories to act in a manner inconsistent with the provisions of Article 2.

3.5   Members are fully responsible under this Agreement for the observance of all provisions of Article 2. Members shall formulate and implement positive measures and mechanisms in support of the observance of the provisions of Article 2 by other than central government bodies.

Article 4

Preparation, Adoption and Application of Standards

4.1   Members shall ensure that their central government standardizing bodies accept and comply with the Code of Good Practice for the Preparation, Adoption and Application of Standards in Annex 3 to this Agreement (referred to in this Agreement as the 'Code of Good Practice'). They shall take such reasonable measures as may be available to them to ensure that local government and non-governmental standardizing bodies within their territories, as well as regional standardizing bodies of which they or one or more bodies within their territories are members, accept and comply with this Code of Good Practice. In addition, Members shall not take measures which have the effect of, directly or indirectly, requiring or encouraging such standardizing bodies to act in a manner inconsistent with the Code of Good Practice. The obligations of Members with respect to compliance of standardizing bodies with the provisions of the Code of Good Practice shall apply irrespective of whether or not a standardizing body has accepted the Code of Good Practice.

4.2   Standardizing bodies that have accepted and are complying with the Code of Good Practice shall be acknowledged by the Members as complying with the principles of this Agreement.

CONFORMITY WITH TECHNICAL REGULATIONS AND STANDARDS

Article 5

Procedures for Assessment of Conformity by Central Government Bodies

5.1   Members shall ensure that, in cases where a positive assurance of conformity with technical regulations or standards is required, their central government bodies apply the following provisions to products originating in the territories of other Members:

> 5.1.1   conformity assessment procedures are prepared, adopted and applied so as to grant access for suppliers of like products originating in the territories of other Members under conditions no less favourable than those accorded to suppliers of like products of national origin or originating in any other country, in a comparable situation; access entails suppliers' right to an assessment of conformity under the rules of the procedure, including, when foreseen by this procedure, the possibility to have conformity assessment activities undertaken at the site of facilities and to receive the mark of the system;

> 5.1.2   conformity assessment procedures are not prepared, adopted or applied with a view to or with the effect of creating unnecessary obstacles to international trade. This means, *inter alia*, that conformity assessment procedures shall not be more strict or be applied more strictly than is necessary to give the importing Member adequate confidence that products conform with the applicable technical regulations or standards, taking account of the risks non-conformity would create.

5.2   When implementing the provisions of paragraph 1, Members shall ensure that:

> 5.2.1   conformity assessment procedures are undertaken and completed as expeditiously as possible and in a no less favourable order for products originating in the territories of other Members than for like domestic products;

> 5.2.2   the standard processing period of each conformity assessment procedure is published or that the anticipated processing period is communicated to the applicant upon request; when receiving an application, the competent body promptly examines the completeness of the documentation and informs the applicant in a precise and complete manner of all deficiencies; the competent body transmits as soon as possible the results of the assessment in a precise and complete manner to the applicant so that corrective action may be taken if necessary; even when the application has deficiencies, the competent body proceeds as far as practicable with the conformity assessment if the applicant so requests; and that, upon request, the applicant is informed of the stage of the procedure, with any delay being explained;

> 5.2.3   information requirements are limited to what is necessary to assess conformity and determine fees;

5.2.4 the confidentiality of information about products originating in the territories of other Members arising from or supplied in connection with such conformity assessment procedures is respected in the same way as for domestic products and in such a manner that legitimate commercial interests are protected;

5.2.5 any fees imposed for assessing the conformity of products originating in the territories of other Members are equitable in relation to any fees chargeable for assessing the conformity of like products of national origin or originating in any other country, taking into account communication, transportation and other costs arising from differences between location of facilities of the applicant and the conformity assessment body;

5.2.6 the siting of facilities used in conformity assessment procedures and the selection of samples are not such as to cause unnecessary inconvenience to applicants or their agents;

5.2.7 whenever specifications of a product are changed subsequent to the determination of its conformity to the applicable technical regulations or standards, the conformity assessment procedure for the modified product is limited to what is necessary to determine whether adequate confidence exists that the product still meets the technical regulations or standards concerned;

5.2.8 a procedure exists to review complaints concerning the operation of a conformity assessment procedure and to take corrective action when a complaint is justified.

5.3 Nothing in paragraphs 1 and 2 shall prevent Members from carrying out reasonable spot checks within their territories.

5.4 In cases where a positive assurance is required that products conform with technical regulations or standards, and relevant guides or recommendations issued by international standardizing bodies exist or their completion is imminent, Members shall ensure that central government bodies use them, or the relevant parts of them, as a basis for their conformity assessment procedures, except where, as duly explained upon request, such guides or recommendations or relevant parts are inappropriate for the Members concerned, for, *inter alia*, such reasons as: national security requirements; the prevention of deceptive practices; protection of human health or safety, animal or plant life or health, or the environment; fundamental climatic or other geographical factors; fundamental technological or infrastructural problems.

5.5 With a view to harmonizing conformity assessment procedures on as wide a basis as possible, Members shall play a full part, within the limits of their resources, in the preparation by appropriate international standardizing bodies of guides and recommendations for conformity assessment procedures.

5.6 Whenever a relevant guide or recommendation issued by an international standardizing body does not exist or the technical content of a proposed conformity assessment procedure is not in accordance with relevant guides and recommendations issued by international standardizing bodies, and if the conformity assessment procedure may have a significant effect on trade of other Members, Members shall:

5.6.1 publish a notice in a publication at an early appropriate stage, in such a manner as to enable interested parties in other Members to become acquainted with it, that they propose to introduce a particular conformity assessment procedure;

5.6.2   notify other Members through the Secretariat of the products to be covered by the proposed conformity assessment procedure, together with a brief indication of its objective and rationale. Such notifications shall take place at an early appropriate stage, when amendments can still be introduced and comments taken into account;

5.6.3   upon request, provide to other Members particulars or copies of the proposed procedure and, whenever possible, identify the parts which in substance deviate from relevant guides or recommendations issued by international standardizing bodies;

5.6.4   without discrimination, allow reasonable time for other Members to make comments in writing, discuss these comments upon request, and take these written comments and the results of these discussions into account.

5.7   Subject to the provisions in the lead-in to paragraph 6, where urgent problems of safety, health, environmental protection or national security arise or threaten to arise for a Member, that Member may omit such of the steps enumerated in paragraph 6 as it finds necessary, provided that the Member, upon adoption of the procedure, shall:

5.7.1   notify immediately other Members through the Secretariat of the particular procedure and the products covered, with a brief indication of the objective and the rationale of the procedure, including the nature of the urgent problems;

5.7.2   upon request, provide other Members with copies of the rules of the procedure;

5.7.3   without discrimination, allow other Members to present their comments in writing, discuss these comments upon request, and take these written comments and the results of these discussions into account.

5.8   Members shall ensure that all conformity assessment procedures which have been adopted are published promptly or otherwise made available in such a manner as to enable interested parties in other Members to become acquainted with them.

5.9   Except in those urgent circumstances referred to in paragraph 7, Members shall allow a reasonable interval between the publication of requirements concerning conformity assessment procedures and their entry into force in order to allow time for producers in exporting Members, and particularly in developing country Members, to adapt their products or methods of production to the requirements of the importing Member.

Article 6

Recognition of Conformity Assessment by Central Government Bodies

With respect to their central government bodies:

6.1   Without prejudice to the provisions of paragraphs 3 and 4, Members shall ensure, whenever possible, that results of conformity assessment procedures in other Members are accepted, even when those procedures differ from their own, provided they are satisfied that those procedures offer an assurance of conformity with applicable technical regulations or standards equivalent to their own procedures. It is recognized that prior consultations may be necessary in order to arrive at a mutually satisfactory understanding regarding, in particular:

6.1.1 adequate and enduring technical competence of the relevant conformity assessment bodies in the exporting Member, so that confidence in the continued reliability of their conformity assessment results can exist; in this regard, verified compliance, for instance through accreditation, with relevant guides or recommendations issued by international standardizing bodies shall be taken into account as an indication of adequate technical competence;

6.1.2 limitation of the acceptance of conformity assessment results to those produced by designated bodies in the exporting Member.

6.2 Members shall ensure that their conformity assessment procedures permit, as far as practicable, the implementation of the provisions in paragraph 1.

6.3 Members are encouraged, at the request of other Members, to be willing to enter into negotiations for the conclusion of agreements for the mutual recognition of results of each other's conformity assessment procedures. Members may require that such agreements fulfil the criteria of paragraph 1 and give mutual satisfaction regarding their potential for facilitating trade in the products concerned.

6.4 Members are encouraged to permit participation of conformity assessment bodies located in the territories of other Members in their conformity assessment procedures under conditions no less favourable than those accorded to bodies located within their territory or the territory of any other country.

Article 7

Procedures for Assessment of Conformity by Local Government Bodies

With respect to their local government bodies within their territories:

7.1 Members shall take such reasonable measures as may be available to them to ensure compliance by such bodies with the provisions of Articles 5 and 6, with the exception of the obligation to notify as referred to in paragraphs 6.2 and 7.1 of Article 5.

7.2 Members shall ensure that the conformity assessment procedures of local governments on the level directly below that of the central government in Members are notified in accordance with the provisions of paragraphs 6.2 and 7.1 of Article 5, noting that notifications shall not be required for conformity assessment procedures the technical content of which is substantially the same as that of previously notified conformity assessment procedures of central government bodies of the Members concerned.

7.3 Members may require contact with other Members, including the notifications, provision of information, comments and discussions referred to in paragraphs 6 and 7 of Article 5, to take place through the central government.

7.4 Members shall not take measures which require or encourage local government bodies within their territories to act in a manner inconsistent with the provisions of Articles 5 and 6.

7.5 Members are fully responsible under this Agreement for the observance of all provisions of Articles 5 and 6. Members shall formulate and implement positive measures and mechanisms in support of the observance of the provisions of Articles 5 and 6 by other than central government bodies.

Article 8

Procedures for Assessment of Conformity by Non-Governmental Bodies

8.1   Members shall take such reasonable measures as may be available to them to ensure that non-governmental bodies within their territories which operate conformity assessment procedures comply with the provisions of Articles 5 and 6, with the exception of the obligation to notify proposed conformity assessment procedures. In addition, Members shall not take measures which have the effect of, directly or indirectly, requiring or encouraging such bodies to act in a manner inconsistent with the provisions of Articles 5 and 6.

8.2   Members shall ensure that their central government bodies rely on conformity assessment procedures operated by non-governmental bodies only if these latter bodies comply with the provisions of Articles 5 and 6, with the exception of the obligation to notify proposed conformity assessment procedures.

Article 9

International and Regional Systems

9.1   Where a positive assurance of conformity with a technical regulation or standard is required, Members shall, wherever practicable, formulate and adopt international systems for conformity assessment and become members thereof or participate therein.

9.2   Members shall take such reasonable measures as may be available to them to ensure that international and regional systems for conformity assessment in which relevant bodies within their territories are members or participants comply with the provisions of Articles 5 and 6. In addition, Members shall not take any measures which have the effect of, directly or indirectly, requiring or encouraging such systems to act in a manner inconsistent with any of the provisions of Articles 5 and 6.

9.3   Members shall ensure that their central government bodies rely on international or regional conformity assessment systems only to the extent that these systems comply with the provisions of Articles 5 and 6, as applicable.

INFORMATION AND ASSISTANCE

Article 10

Information About Technical Regulations, Standards and Conformity Assessment Procedures

10.1   Each Member shall ensure that an enquiry point exists which is able to answer all reasonable enquiries from other Members and interested parties in other Members as well as to provide the relevant documents regarding:

10.1.1 any technical regulations adopted or proposed within its territory by central or local government bodies, by non-governmental bodies which have legal power to enforce a technical regulation, or by regional standardizing bodies of which such bodies are members or participants;

10.1.2 any standards adopted or proposed within its territory by central or local government bodies, or by regional standardizing bodies of which such bodies are members or participants;

10.1.3 any conformity assessment procedures, or proposed conformity assessment procedures, which are operated within its territory by central or local government bodies, or by non-governmental bodies which have legal power to enforce a technical regulation, or by regional bodies of which such bodies are members or participants;

10.1.4 the membership and participation of the Member, or of relevant central or local government bodies within its territory, in international and regional standardizing bodies and conformity assessment systems, as well as in bilateral and multilateral arrangements within the scope of this Agreement; it shall also be able to provide reasonable information on the provisions of such systems and arrangements;

10.1.5 the location of notices published pursuant to this Agreement, or the provision of information as to where such information can be obtained; and

10.1.6 the location of the enquiry points mentioned in paragraph 3.

10.2   If, however, for legal or administrative reasons more than one enquiry point is established by a Member, that Member shall provide to the other Members complete and unambiguous information on the scope of responsibility of each of these enquiry points. In addition, that Member shall ensure that any enquiries addressed to an incorrect enquiry point shall promptly be conveyed to the correct enquiry point.

10.3   Each Member shall take such reasonable measures as may be available to it to ensure that one or more enquiry points exist which are able to answer all reasonable enquiries from other Members and interested parties in other Members as well as to provide the relevant documents or information as to where they can be obtained regarding:

10.3.1 any standards adopted or proposed within its territory by non-governmental standardizing bodies, or by regional standardizing bodies of which such bodies are members or participants; and

10.3.2 any conformity assessment procedures, or proposed conformity assessment procedures, which are operated within its territory by non-governmental bodies, or by regional bodies of which such bodies are members or participants;

10.3.3 the membership and participation of relevant non-governmental bodies within its territory in international and regional standardizing bodies and conformity assessment systems, as well as in bilateral and multilateral arrangements within the scope of this Agreement; they shall also be able to provide reasonable information on the provisions of such systems and arrangements.

10.4   Members shall take such reasonable measures as may be available to them to ensure that where copies of documents are requested by other Members or by interested parties in other Members, in accordance with the provisions of this Agreement, they are supplied at an equitable price (if any) which shall, apart from the real cost of delivery, be the same for the nationals* of the Member concerned or of any other Member.

---

*   'Nationals' here shall be deemed, in the case of a separate customs territory Member of the WTO, to mean persons, natural or legal, who are domiciled or who have a real and effective industrial or commercial establishment in that customs territory.

10.5   Developed country Members shall, if requested by other Members, provide, in English, French or Spanish, translations of the documents covered by a specific notification or, in case of voluminous documents, of summaries of such documents.

10.6   The Secretariat shall, when it receives notifications in accordance with the provisions of this Agreement, circulate copies of the notifications to all Members and interested international standardizing and conformity assessment bodies, and draw the attention of developing country Members to any notifications relating to products of particular interest to them.

10.7   Whenever a Member has reached an agreement with any other country or countries on issues related to technical regulations, standards or conformity assessment procedures which may have a significant effect on trade, at least one Member party to the agreement shall notify other Members through the Secretariat of the products to be covered by the agreement and include a brief description of the agreement. Members concerned are encouraged to enter, upon request, into consultations with other Members for the purposes of concluding similar agreements or of arranging for their participation in such agreements.

10.8   Nothing in this Agreement shall be construed as requiring:

> 10.8.1 the publication of texts other than in the language of the Member;
>
> 10.8.2 the provision of particulars or copies of drafts other than in the language of the Member except as stated in paragraph 5; or
>
> 10.8.3 Members to furnish any information, the disclosure of which they consider contrary to their essential security interests.

10.9   Notifications to the Secretariat shall be in English, French or Spanish.

10.10   Members shall designate a single central government authority that is responsible for the implementation on the national level of the provisions concerning notification procedures under this Agreement except those included in Annex 3.

10.11   If, however, for legal or administrative reasons the responsibility for notification procedures is divided among two or more central government authorities, the Member concerned shall provide to the other Members complete and unambiguous information on the scope of responsibility of each of these authorities.

Article 11

Technical Assistance to Other Members

11.1   Members shall, if requested, advise other Members, especially the developing country Members, on the preparation of technical regulations.

11.2   Members shall, if requested, advise other Members, especially the developing country Members, and shall grant them technical assistance on mutually agreed terms and conditions regarding the establishment of national standardizing bodies, and participation in the international standardizing bodies, and shall encourage their national standardizing bodies to do likewise.

11.3   Members shall, if requested, take such reasonable measures as may be available to them to arrange for the regulatory bodies within their territories to advise other Members, especially the developing country Members, and shall grant them technical assistance on mutually agreed terms and conditions regarding:

11.3.1 the establishment of regulatory bodies, or bodies for the assessment of conformity with technical regulations; and

11.3.2 the methods by which their technical regulations can best be met.

11.4   Members shall, if requested, take such reasonable measures as may be available to them to arrange for advice to be given to other Members, especially the developing country Members, and shall grant them technical assistance on mutually agreed terms and conditions regarding the establishment of bodies for the assessment of conformity with standards adopted within the territory of the requesting Member.

11.5   Members shall, if requested, advise other Members, especially the developing country Members, and shall grant them technical assistance on mutually agreed terms and conditions regarding the steps that should be taken by their producers if they wish to have access to systems for conformity assessment operated by governmental or non-governmental bodies within the territory of the Member receiving the request.

11.6   Members which are members or participants of international or regional systems for conformity assessment shall, if requested, advise other Members, especially the developing country Members, and shall grant them technical assistance on mutually agreed terms and conditions regarding the establishment of the institutions and legal framework which would enable them to fulfil the obligations of membership or participation in such systems.

11.7   Members shall, if so requested, encourage bodies within their territories which are members or participants of international or regional systems for conformity assessment to advise other Members, especially the developing country Members, and should consider requests for technical assistance from them regarding the establishment of the institutions which would enable the relevant bodies within their territories to fulfil the obligations of membership or participation.

11.8   In providing advice and technical assistance to other Members in terms of paragraphs 1 to 7, Members shall give priority to the needs of the least-developed country Members.

Article 12

Special and Differential Treatment of Developing Country Members

12.1   Members shall provide differential and more favourable treatment to developing country Members to this Agreement, through the following provisions as well as through the relevant provisions of other Articles of this Agreement.

12.2   Members shall give particular attention to the provisions of this Agreement concerning developing country Members' rights and obligations and shall take into account the special development, financial and trade needs of developing country Members in the implementation of this Agreement, both nationally and in the operation of this Agreement's institutional arrangements.

12.3   Members shall, in the preparation and application of technical regulations, standards and conformity assessment procedures, take account of the special development, financial and trade needs of developing country Members, with a view to ensuring that such technical regulations, standards and conformity assessment procedures do not create unnecessary obstacles to exports from developing country Members.

12.4   Members recognize that, although international standards, guides or recommendations may exist, in their particular technological and socio-economic conditions, developing country Members adopt certain technical regulations, standards or conformity assessment procedures aimed at preserving indigenous technology and production methods and processes compatible with their development needs. Members therefore recognize that developing country Members should not be expected to use international standards as a basis for their technical regulations or standards, including test methods, which are not appropriate to their development, financial and trade needs.

12.5   Members shall take such reasonable measures as may be available to them to ensure that international standardizing bodies and international systems for conformity assessment are organized and operated in a way which facilitates active and representative participation of relevant bodies in all Members, taking into account the special problems of developing country Members.

12.6   Members shall take such reasonable measures as may be available to them to ensure that international standardizing bodies, upon request of developing country Members, examine the possibility of, and, if practicable, prepare international standards concerning products of special interest to developing country Members.

12.7   Members shall, in accordance with the provisions of Article 11, provide technical assistance to developing country Members to ensure that the preparation and application of technical regulations, standards and conformity assessment procedures do not create unnecessary obstacles to the expansion and diversification of exports from developing country Members. In determining the terms and conditions of the technical assistance, account shall be taken of the stage of development of the requesting Members and in particular of the least-developed country Members.

12.8   It is recognized that developing country Members may face special problems, including institutional and infrastructural problems, in the field of preparation and application of technical regulations, standards and conformity assessment procedures. It is further recognized that the special development and trade needs of developing country Members, as well as their stage of technological development, may hinder their ability to discharge fully their obligations under this Agreement. Members, therefore, shall take this fact fully into account. Accordingly, with a view to ensuring that developing country Members are able to comply with this Agreement, the Committee on Technical Barriers to Trade provided for in Article 13 (referred to in this Agreement as the 'Committee') is enabled to grant, upon request, specified, time-limited exceptions in whole or in part from obligations under this Agreement. When considering such requests the Committee shall take into account the special problems, in the field of preparation and application of technical regulations, standards and conformity assessment procedures, and the special development and trade needs of the developing country Member, as well as its stage of technological development, which may hinder its ability to discharge fully its obligations under this Agreement. The Committee shall, in particular, take into account the special problems of the least-developed country Members.

12.9   During consultations, developed country Members shall bear in mind the special difficulties experienced by developing country Members in formulating and implementing standards and technical regulations and conformity assessment procedures, and in their desire to assist developing country Members with their efforts in this direction, developed country Members shall take account of the special needs of the former in regard to financing, trade and development.

12.10   The Committee shall examine periodically the special and differential treatment, as laid down in this Agreement, granted to developing country Members on national and international levels.

INSTITUTIONS, CONSULTATION AND DISPUTE SETTLEMENT

Article 13

The Committee on Technical Barriers to Trade

13.1   A Committee on Technical Barriers to Trade is hereby established, and shall be composed of representatives from each of the Members. The Committee shall elect its own Chairman and shall meet as necessary, but no less than once a year, for the purpose of affording Members the opportunity of consulting on any matters relating to the operation of this Agreement or the furtherance of its objectives, and shall carry out such responsibilities as assigned to it under this Agreement or by the Members.

13.2   The Committee shall establish working parties or other bodies as may be appropriate, which shall carry out such responsibilities as may be assigned to them by the Committee in accordance with the relevant provisions of this Agreement.

13.3   It is understood that unnecessary duplication should be avoided between the work under this Agreement and that of governments in other technical bodies. The Committee shall examine this problem with a view to minimizing such duplication.

Article 14

Consultation and Dispute Settlement

14.1   Consultations and the settlement of disputes with respect to any matter affecting the operation of this Agreement shall take place under the auspices of the Dispute Settlement Body and shall follow, *mutatis mutandis*, the provisions of Articles XXII and XXIII of GATT 1994, as elaborated and applied by the Dispute Settlement Understanding.

14.2   At the request of a party to a dispute, or at its own initiative, a panel may establish a technical expert group to assist in questions of a technical nature, requiring detailed consideration by experts.

14.3   Technical expert groups shall be governed by the procedures of Annex 2.

14.4   The dispute settlement provisions set out above can be invoked in cases where a Member considers that another Member has not achieved satisfactory results under Articles 3, 4, 7, 8 and 9 and its trade interests are significantly affected. In this respect, such results shall be equivalent to those as if the body in question were a Member.

FINAL PROVISIONS

Article 15

Final Provisions

Reservations

15.1   Reservations may not be entered in respect of any of the provisions of this Agreement without the consent of the other Members.

Review

15.2   Each Member shall, promptly after the date on which the WTO Agreement enters into force for it, inform the Committee of measures in existence or taken to ensure the implementation and administration of this Agreement. Any changes of such measures thereafter shall also be notified to the Committee.

15.3   The Committee shall review annually the implementation and operation of this Agreement taking into account the objectives thereof.

15.4   Not later than the end of the third year from the date of entry into force of the WTO Agreement and at the end of each three-year period thereafter, the Committee shall review the operation and implementation of this Agreement, including the provisions relating to transparency, with a view to recommending an adjustment of the rights and obligations of this Agreement where necessary to ensure mutual economic advantage and balance of rights and obligations, without prejudice to the provisions of Article 12. Having regard, *inter alia,* to the experience gained in the implementation of the Agreement, the Committee shall, where appropriate, submit proposals for amendments to the text of this Agreement to the Council for Trade in Goods.

Annexes

15.5   The annexes to this Agreement constitute an integral part thereof.

ANNEX 1

TERMS AND THEIR DEFINITIONS FOR THE PURPOSE OF THIS AGREEMENT

The terms presented in the sixth edition of the ISO/IEC Guide 2: 1991, General Terms and Their Definitions Concerning Standardization and Related Activities, shall, when used in this Agreement, have the same meaning as given in the definitions in the said Guide taking into account that services are excluded from the coverage of this Agreement.

For the purpose of this Agreement, however, the following definitions shall apply:

1.   *Technical regulation*

Document which lays down product characteristics or their related processes and production methods, including the applicable administrative provisions, with which compliance is mandatory. It may also include or deal exclusively with terminology, symbols, packaging, marking or labelling requirements as they apply to a product, process or production method.

Explanatory note

The definition in ISO/IEC Guide 2 is not self-contained, but based on the so-called 'building block' system.

2.   *Standard*

Document approved by a recognized body, that provides, for common and repeated use, rules, guidelines or characteristics for products or related processes and production methods, with which compliance is not mandatory. It may also include or deal exclusively with terminology, symbols, packaging, marking or labelling requirements as they apply to a product, process or production method.

Explanatory note

The terms as defined in ISO/IEC Guide 2 cover products, processes and services. This Agreement deals only with technical regulations, standards and conformity assessment procedures related to products or processes and production methods. Standards as defined by ISO/IEC Guide 2 may be mandatory or voluntary. For the purpose of this Agreement standards are defined as voluntary and technical regulations as mandatory documents. Standards prepared by the international standardization community are based on consensus. This Agreement covers also documents that are not based on consensus.

3. *Conformity assessment procedures*

Any procedure used, directly or indirectly, to determine that relevant requirements in technical regulations or standards are fulfilled.

Explanatory note

Conformity assessment procedures include, *inter alia*, procedures for sampling, testing and inspection; evaluation, verification and assurance of conformity; registration, accreditation and approval as well as their combinations.

4. *International body or system*

Body or system whose membership is open to the relevant bodies of at least all Members.

5. *Regional body or system*

Body or system whose membership is open to the relevant bodies of only some of the Members.

6. *Central government body*

Central government, its ministries and departments or any body subject to the control of the central government in respect of the activity in question.

Explanatory note:

In the case of the European Communities the provisions governing central government bodies apply. However, regional bodies or conformity assessment systems may be established within the European Communities, and in such cases would be subject to the provisions of this Agreement on regional bodies or conformity assessment systems.

7. *Local government body*

Government other than a central government (e.g. states, provinces, Länder, cantons, municipalities, etc.), its ministries or departments or any body subject to the control of such a government in respect of the activity in question.

8. *Non-governmental body*

Body other than a central government body or a local government body, including a non-governmental body which has legal power to enforce a technical regulation.

ANNEX 2

TECHNICAL EXPERT GROUPS

The following procedures shall apply to technical expert groups established in accordance with the provisions of Article 14.

1.   Technical expert groups are under the panel's authority. Their terms of reference and detailed working procedures shall be decided by the panel, and they shall report to the panel.

2.   Participation in technical expert groups shall be restricted to persons of professional standing and experience in the field in question.

3.   Citizens of parties to the dispute shall not serve on a technical expert group without the joint agreement of the parties to the dispute, except in exceptional circumstances when the panel considers that the need for specialized scientific expertise cannot be fulfilled otherwise. Government officials of parties to the dispute shall not serve on a technical expert group. Members of technical expert groups shall serve in their individual capacities and not as government representatives, nor as representatives of any organization. Governments or organizations shall therefore not give them instructions with regard to matters before a technical expert group.

4.   Technical expert groups may consult and seek information and technical advice from any source they deem appropriate. Before a technical expert group seeks such information or advice from a source within the jurisdiction of a Member, it shall inform the government of that Member. Any Member shall respond promptly and fully to any request by a technical expert group for such information as the technical expert group considers necessary and appropriate.

5.   The parties to a dispute shall have access to all relevant information provided to a technical expert group, unless it is of a confidential nature. Confidential information provided to the technical expert group shall not be released without formal authorization from the government, organization or person providing the information. Where such information is requested from the technical expert group but release of such information by the technical expert group is not authorized, a non-confidential summary of the information will be provided by the government, organization or person supplying the information.

6.   The technical expert group shall submit a draft report to the Members concerned with a view to obtaining their comments, and taking them into account, as appropriate, in the final report, which shall also be circulated to the Members concerned when it is submitted to the panel.

ANNEX 3

CODE OF GOOD PRACTICE FOR THE PREPARATION, ADOPTION AND APPLICATION OF STANDARDS

General Provisions

A.   For the purposes of this Code the definitions in Annex 1 of this Agreement shall apply.

B.   This Code is open to acceptance by any standardizing body within the territory of a Member of the WTO, whether a central government body, a local government body, or a non-governmental body; to any governmental regional standardizing body one or more members of which are Members of the WTO; and to any non-governmental regional standardizing body one or more members of which are situated within the territory of a Member of the WTO (referred to in this Code collectively as 'standardizing bodies' and individually as 'the standardizing body').

C.   Standardizing bodies that have accepted or withdrawn from this Code shall notify this fact to the ISO/IEC Information Centre in Geneva. The notification shall include the name and address of the body concerned and the scope of its current and expected standardization activities. The notification may be sent either directly to the ISO/IEC Information Centre, or through the national member body of ISO/IEC or, preferably, through the relevant national member or international affiliate of ISONET, as appropriate.

SUBSTANTIVE PROVISIONS

D.   In respect of standards, the standardizing body shall accord treatment to products originating in the territory of any other Member of the WTO no less favourable than that accorded to like products of national origin and to like products originating in any other country.

E.   The standardizing body shall ensure that standards are not prepared, adopted or applied with a view to, or with the effect of, creating unnecessary obstacles to international trade.

F.   Where international standards exist or their completion is imminent, the standardizing body shall use them, or the relevant parts of them, as a basis for the standards it develops, except where such international standards or relevant parts would be ineffective or inappropriate, for instance, because of an insufficient level of protection or fundamental climatic or geographical factors or fundamental technological problems.

G.   With a view to harmonizing standards on as wide a basis as possible, the standardizing body shall, in an appropriate way, play a full part, within the limits of its resources, in the preparation by relevant international standardizing bodies of international standards regarding subject matter for which it either has adopted, or expects to adopt, standards. For standardizing bodies within the territory of a Member, participation in a particular international standardization activity shall, whenever possible, take place through one delegation representing all standardizing bodies in the territory that have adopted, or expect to adopt, standards for the subject matter to which the international standardization activity relates.

H.   The standardizing body within the territory of a Member shall make every effort to avoid duplication of, or overlap with, the work of other standardizing bodies in the national territory or with the work of relevant international or regional standardizing bodies. They shall also make every effort to achieve a national consensus on the standards they develop. Likewise the regional standardizing body shall make every effort to avoid duplication of, or overlap with, the work of relevant international standardizing bodies.

I.   Wherever appropriate, the standardizing body shall specify standards based on product requirements in terms of performance rather than design or descriptive characteristics.

J.   At least once every six months, the standardizing body shall publish a work programme containing its name and address, the standards it is currently preparing and the standards which it has adopted in the preceding period. A standard is under preparation from the moment a decision has been taken to develop a standard until that standard has been adopted. The titles of specific draft standards shall, upon request, be provided in English, French or Spanish. A notice of the existence of the work programme shall be published in a national or, as the case may be, regional publication of standardization activities.

The work programme shall for each standard indicate, in accordance with any ISONET rules, the classification relevant to the subject matter, the stage attained in the standard's development, and the references of any international standards taken as a basis. No later than at the time of publication of its work programme, the standardizing body shall notify the existence thereof to the ISO/IEC Information Centre in Geneva.

The notification shall contain the name and address of the standardizing body, the name and issue of the publication in which the work programme is published, the period to which the work programme applies, its price (if any), and how and where it can be obtained. The notification may be sent directly to the ISO/IEC Information Centre, or, preferably, through the relevant national member or international affiliate of ISONET, as appropriate.

K.   The national member of ISO/IEC shall make every effort to become a member of ISONET or to appoint another body to become a member as well as to acquire the most advanced membership type possible for the ISONET member. Other standardizing bodies shall make every effort to associate themselves with the ISONET member.

L.   Before adopting a standard, the standardizing body shall allow a period of at least 60 days for the submission of comments on the draft standard by interested parties within the territory of a Member of the WTO. This period may, however, be shortened in cases where urgent problems of safety, health or environment arise or threaten to arise. No later than at the start of the comment period, the standardizing body shall publish a notice announcing the period for commenting in the publication referred to in paragraph J. Such notification shall include, as far as practicable, whether the draft standard deviates from relevant international standards.

M.   On the request of any interested party within the territory of a Member of the WTO, the standardizing body shall promptly provide, or arrange to provide, a copy of a draft standard which it has submitted for comments. Any fees charged for this service shall, apart from the real cost of delivery, be the same for foreign and domestic parties.

N.   The standardizing body shall take into account, in the further processing of the standard, the comments received during the period for commenting. Comments received through standardizing bodies that have accepted this Code of Good Practice shall, if so requested, be replied to as promptly as possible. The reply shall include an explanation why a deviation from relevant international standards is necessary.

O.   Once the standard has been adopted, it shall be promptly published.

P.   On the request of any interested party within the territory of a Member of the WTO, the standardizing body shall promptly provide, or arrange to provide, a copy of its most recent work programme or of a standard which it produced. Any fees charged for this service shall, apart from the real cost of delivery, be the same for foreign and domestic parties.

Q.   The standardizing body shall afford sympathetic consideration to, and adequate opportunity for, consultation regarding representations with respect to the operation of this Code presented by standardizing bodies that have accepted this Code of Good Practice. It shall make an objective effort to solve any complaints.

Agreement on the Application of Sanitary and Phytosanitary Measures

Members,

Reaffirming that no Member should be prevented from adopting or enforcing measures necessary to protect human, animal or plant life or health, subject to the requirement that these measures are not applied in a manner which would constitute a means of arbitrary or unjustifiable discrimination between Members where the same conditions prevail or a disguised restriction on international trade;

Desiring to improve the human health, animal health and phytosanitary situation in all Members;

Noting that sanitary and phytosanitary measures are often applied on the basis of bilateral agreements or protocols;

Desiring the establishment of a multilateral framework of rules and disciplines to guide the development, adoption and enforcement of sanitary and phytosanitary measures in order to minimize their negative effects on trade;

Recognizing the important contribution that international standards, guidelines and recommendations can make in this regard;

Desiring to further the use of harmonized sanitary and phytosanitary measures between Members, on the basis of international standards, guidelines and recommendations developed by the relevant international organizations, including the Codex Alimentarius Commission, the International Office of Epizootics, and the relevant international and regional organizations operating within the framework of the International Plant Protection Convention, without requiring Members to change their appropriate level of protection of human, animal or plant life or health;

Recognizing that developing country Members may encounter special difficulties in complying with the sanitary or phytosanitary measures of importing Members, and as a consequence in access to markets, and also in the formulation and application of sanitary or phytosanitary measures in their own territories, and desiring to assist them in their endeavours in this regard;

Desiring therefore to elaborate rules for the application of the provisions of GATT 1994 which relate to the use of sanitary or phytosanitary measures, in particular the provisions of Article XX(b);

Hereby agree as follows:

Article 1

General Provisions

1.   This Agreement applies to all sanitary and phytosanitary measures which may, directly or indirectly, affect international trade. Such measures shall be developed and applied in accordance with the provisions of this Agreement.

2.   For the purposes of this Agreement, the definitions provided in Annex A shall apply.

3.   The annexes are an integral part of this Agreement.

4.   Nothing in this Agreement shall affect the rights of Members under the Agreement on Technical Barriers to Trade with respect to measures not within the scope of this Agreement.

Article 2

Basic Rights and Obligations

1.   Members have the right to take sanitary and phytosanitary measures necessary for the protection of human, animal or plant life or health, provided that such measures are not inconsistent with the provisions of this Agreement.

2.   Members shall ensure that any sanitary or phytosanitary measure is applied only to the extent necessary to protect human, animal or plant life or health, is based on scientific principles and is not maintained without sufficient scientific evidence, except as provided for in paragraph 7 of Article 5.

3.   Members shall ensure that their sanitary and phytosanitary measures do not arbitrarily or unjustifiably discriminate between Members where identical or similar conditions prevail, including between their own territory and that of other Members. Sanitary and phytosanitary measures shall not be applied in a manner which would constitute a disguised restriction on international trade.

4.   Sanitary or phytosanitary measures which conform to the relevant provisions of this Agreement shall be presumed to be in accordance with the obligations of the Members under the provisions of GATT 1994 which relate to the use of sanitary or phytosanitary measures, in particular the provisions of Article XX(b).

Article 3

Harmonization

1.   To harmonize sanitary and phytosanitary measures on as wide a basis as possible, Members shall base their sanitary or phytosanitary measures on international standards, guidelines or recommendations, where they exist, except as otherwise provided for in this Agreement, and in particular in paragraph 3.

2.   Sanitary or phytosanitary measures which conform to international standards, guidelines or recommendations shall be deemed to be necessary to protect human, animal or plant life or health, and presumed to be consistent with the relevant provisions of this Agreement and of GATT 1994.

3.   Members may introduce or maintain sanitary or phytosanitary measures which result in a higher level of sanitary or phytosanitary protection than would be achieved by measures based on the relevant international

standards, guidelines or recommendations, if there is a scientific justification, or as a consequence of the level of sanitary or phytosanitary protection a Member determines to be appropriate in accordance with the relevant provisions of paragraphs 1 through 8 of Article 5. Notwithstanding the above, all measures which result in a level of sanitary or phytosanitary protection different from that which would be achieved by measures based on international standards, guidelines or recommendations shall not be inconsistent with any other provision of this Agreement.

4.   Members shall play a full part, within the limits of their resources, in the relevant international organizations and their subsidiary bodies, in particular the Codex Alimentarius Commission, the International Office of Epizootics, and the international and regional organizations operating within the framework of the International Plant Protection Convention, to promote within these organizations the development and periodic review of standards, guidelines and recommendations with respect to all aspects of sanitary and phytosanitary measures.

5.   The Committee on Sanitary and Phytosanitary Measures provided for in paragraphs 1 and 4 of Article 12 (referred to in this Agreement as the 'Committee') shall develop a procedure to monitor the process of international harmonization and coordinate efforts in this regard with the relevant international organizations.

Article 4

Equivalence

1.   Members shall accept the sanitary or phytosanitary measures of other Members as equivalent, even if these measures differ from their own or from those used by other Members trading in the same product, if the exporting Member objectively demonstrates to the importing Member that its measures achieve the importing Member's appropriate level of sanitary or phytosanitary protection. For this purpose, reasonable access shall be given, upon request, to the importing Member for inspection, testing and other relevant procedures.

2.   Members shall, upon request, enter into consultations with the aim of achieving bilateral and multilateral agreements on recognition of the equivalence of specified sanitary or phytosanitary measures.

Article 5

Assessment of Risk and Determination of the Appropriate Level of Sanitary or Phytosanitary Protection

1.   Members shall ensure that their sanitary or phytosanitary measures are based on an assessment, as appropriate to the circumstances, of the risks to human, animal or plant life or health, taking into account risk assessment techniques developed by the relevant international organizations.

2.   In the assessment of risks, Members shall take into account available scientific evidence; relevant processes and production methods; relevant inspection, sampling and testing methods; prevalence of specific diseases or pests; existence of pest- or disease-free areas; relevant ecological and environmental conditions; and quarantine or other treatment.

3.   In assessing the risk to animal or plant life or health and determining the measure to be applied for achieving the appropriate level of sanitary or phytosanitary protection from such risk, Members shall take into account as relevant economic factors: the potential damage in terms of loss of production

or sales in the event of the entry, establishment or spread of a pest or disease; the costs of control or eradication in the territory of the importing Member; and the relative cost-effectiveness of alternative approaches to limiting risks.

4.   Members should, when determining the appropriate level of sanitary or phytosanitary protection, take into account the objective of minimizing negative trade effects.

5.   With the objective of achieving consistency in the application of the concept of appropriate level of sanitary or phytosanitary protection against risks to human life or health, or to animal and plant life or health, each Member shall avoid arbitrary or unjustifiable distinctions in the levels it considers to be appropriate in different situations, if such distinctions result in discrimination or a disguised restriction on international trade. Members shall cooperate in the Committee, in accordance with paragraphs 1, 2 and 3 of Article 12, to develop guidelines to further the practical implementation of this provision. In developing the guidelines, the Committee shall take into account all relevant factors, including the exceptional character of human health risks to which people voluntarily expose themselves.

6.   Without prejudice to paragraph 2 of Article 3, when establishing or maintaining sanitary or phytosanitary measures to achieve the appropriate level of sanitary or phytosanitary protection, Members shall ensure that such measures are not more trade-restrictive than required to achieve their appropriate level of sanitary or phytosanitary protection, taking into account technical and economic feasibility.

7.   In cases where relevant scientific evidence is insufficient, a Member may provisionally adopt sanitary or phytosanitary measures on the basis of available pertinent information, including that from the relevant international organizations as well as from sanitary or phytosanitary measures applied by other Members. In such circumstances, Members shall seek to obtain the additional information necessary for a more objective assessment of risk and review the sanitary or phytosanitary measure accordingly within a reasonable period of time.

8.   When a Member has reason to believe that a specific sanitary or phytosanitary measure introduced or maintained by another Member is constraining, or has the potential to constrain, its exports and the measure is not based on the relevant international standards, guidelines or recommendations, or such standards, guidelines or recommendations do not exist, an explanation of the reasons for such sanitary or phytosanitary measure may be requested and shall be provided by the Member maintaining the measure.

Article 6

Adaptation to Regional Conditions, Including Pest- or Disease-Free Areas and Areas of Low Pest or Disease Prevalence

1.   Members shall ensure that their sanitary or phytosanitary measures are adapted to the sanitary or phytosanitary characteristics of the area - whether all of a country, part of a country, or all or parts of several countries - from which the product originated and to which the product is destined. In assessing the sanitary or phytosanitary characteristics of a region, Members shall take into account, *inter alia*, the level of prevalence of specific diseases or pests, the existence of eradication or control programmes, and appropriate criteria or guidelines which may be developed by the relevant international organizations.

2.   Members shall, in particular, recognize the concepts of pest- or disease-free areas and areas of low pest or disease prevalence. Determination of

such areas shall be based on factors such as geography, ecosystems, epidemiological surveillance, and the effectiveness of sanitary or phytosanitary controls.

3.   Exporting Members claiming that areas within their territories are pest- or disease-free areas or areas of low pest or disease prevalence shall provide the necessary evidence thereof in order to objectively demonstrate to the importing Member that such areas are, and are likely to remain, pest- or disease-free areas or areas of low pest or disease prevalence, respectively. For this purpose, reasonable access shall be given, upon request, to the importing Member for inspection, testing and other relevant procedures.

Article 7

Transparency

Members shall notify changes in their sanitary or phytosanitary measures and shall provide information on their sanitary or phytosanitary measures in accordance with the provisions of Annex B.

Article 8

Control, Inspection and Approval Procedures

Members shall observe the provisions of Annex C in the operation of control, inspection and approval procedures, including national systems for approving the use of additives or for establishing tolerances for contaminants in foods, beverages or feedstuffs, and otherwise ensure that their procedures are not inconsistent with the provisions of this Agreement.

Article 9

Technical Assistance

1.   Members agree to facilitate the provision of technical assistance to other Members, especially developing country Members, either bilaterally or through the appropriate international organizations. Such assistance may be, *inter alia*, in the areas of processing technologies, research and infrastructure, including in the establishment of national regulatory bodies, and may take the form of advice, credits, donations and grants, including for the purpose of seeking technical expertise, training and equipment to allow such countries to adjust to, and comply with, sanitary or phytosanitary measures necessary to achieve the appropriate level of sanitary or phytosanitary protection in their export markets.

2.   Where substantial investments are required in order for an exporting developing country Member to fulfil the sanitary or phytosanitary requirements of an importing Member, the latter shall consider providing such technical assistance as will permit the developing country Member to maintain and expand its market access opportunities for the product involved.

Article 10

Special and Differential Treatment

1.   In the preparation and application of sanitary or phytosanitary measures, Members shall take account of the special needs of developing country Members, and in particular of the least-developed country Members.

2.   Where the appropriate level of sanitary or phytosanitary protection allows scope for the phased introduction of new sanitary or phytosanitary measures, longer time-frames for compliance should be accorded on products of interest to developing country Members so as to maintain opportunities for their exports.

3.   With a view to ensuring that developing country Members are able to comply with the provisions of this Agreement, the Committee is enabled to grant to such countries, upon request, specified, time-limited exceptions in whole or in part from obligations under this Agreement, taking into account their financial, trade and development needs.

4.   Members should encourage and facilitate the active participation of developing country Members in the relevant international organizations.

Article 11

Consultations and Dispute Settlement

1.   The provisions of Articles XXII and XXIII of GATT 1994 as elaborated and applied by the Dispute Settlement Understanding shall apply to consultations and the settlement of disputes under this Agreement, except as otherwise specifically provided herein.

2.   In a dispute under this Agreement involving scientific or technical issues, a panel should seek advice from experts chosen by the panel in consultation with the parties to the dispute. To this end, the panel may, when it deems it appropriate, establish an advisory technical experts group, or consult the relevant international organizations, at the request of either party to the dispute or on its own initiative.

3.   Nothing in this Agreement shall impair the rights of Members under other international agreements, including the right to resort to the good offices or dispute settlement mechanisms of other international organizations or established under any international agreement.

Article 12

Administration

1.   A Committee on Sanitary and Phytosanitary Measures is hereby established to provide a regular forum for consultations. It shall carry out the functions necessary to implement the provisions of this Agreement and the furtherance of its objectives, in particular with respect to harmonization. The Committee shall reach its decisions by consensus.

2.   The Committee shall encourage and facilitate ad hoc consultations or negotiations among Members on specific sanitary or phytosanitary issues. The Committee shall encourage the use of international standards, guidelines or recommendations by all Members and, in this regard, shall sponsor technical consultation and study with the objective of increasing coordination and integration between international and national systems and approaches for approving the use of food additives or for establishing tolerances for contaminants in foods, beverages or feedstuffs.

3.   The Committee shall maintain close contact with the relevant international organizations in the field of sanitary and phytosanitary protection, especially with the Codex Alimentarius Commission, the International Office of Epizootics, and the Secretariat of the International Plant Protection Convention, with the objective of securing the best available

scientific and technical advice for the administration of this Agreement and in order to ensure that unnecessary duplication of effort is avoided.

4.   The Committee shall develop a procedure to monitor the process of international harmonization and the use of international standards, guidelines or recommendations. For this purpose, the Committee should, in conjunction with the relevant international organizations, establish a list of international standards, guidelines or recommendations relating to sanitary or phytosanitary measures which the Committee determines to have a major trade impact. The list should include an indication by Members of those international standards, guidelines or recommendations which they apply as conditions for import or on the basis of which imported products conforming to these standards can enjoy access to their markets. For those cases in which a Member does not apply an international standard, guideline or recommendation as a condition for import, the Member should provide an indication of the reason therefor, and, in particular, whether it considers that the standard is not stringent enough to provide the appropriate level of sanitary or phytosanitary protection. If a Member revises its position, following its indication of the use of a standard, guideline or recommendation as a condition for import, it should provide an explanation for its change and so inform the Secretariat as well as the relevant international organizations, unless such notification and explanation is given according to the procedures of Annex B.

5.   In order to avoid unnecessary duplication, the Committee may decide, as appropriate, to use the information generated by the procedures, particularly for notification, which are in operation in the relevant international organizations.

6.   The Committee may, on the basis of an initiative from one of the Members, through appropriate channels invite the relevant international organizations or their subsidiary bodies to examine specific matters with respect to a particular standard, guideline or recommendation, including the basis of explanations for non-use given according to paragraph 4.

7.   The Committee shall review the operation and implementation of this Agreement three years after the date of entry into force of the WTO Agreement, and thereafter as the need arises. Where appropriate, the Committee may submit to the Council for Trade in Goods proposals to amend the text of this Agreement having regard, *inter alia*, to the experience gained in its implementation.

Article 13

Implementation

Members are fully responsible under this Agreement for the observance of all obligations set forth herein. Members shall formulate and implement positive measures and mechanisms in support of the observance of the provisions of this Agreement by other than central government bodies. Members shall take such reasonable measures as may be available to them to ensure that non-governmental entities within their territories, as well as regional bodies in which relevant entities within their territories are members, comply with the relevant provisions of this Agreement. In addition, Members shall not take measures which have the effect of, directly or indirectly, requiring or encouraging such regional or non-governmental entities, or local governmental bodies, to act in a manner inconsistent with the provisions of this Agreement. Members shall ensure that they rely on the services of non-governmental entities for implementing sanitary or phytosanitary measures only if these entities comply with the provisions of this Agreement.

Article 14

Final Provisions

The least-developed country Members may delay application of the provisions of this Agreement for a period of five years following the date of entry into force of the WTO Agreement with respect to their sanitary or phytosanitary measures affecting importation or imported products. Other developing country Members may delay application of the provisions of this Agreement, other than paragraph 8 of Article 5 and Article 7, for two years following the date of entry into force of the WTO Agreement with respect to their existing sanitary or phytosanitary measures affecting importation or imported products, where such application is prevented by a lack of technical expertise, technical infrastructure or resources.

ANNEX A

DEFINITIONS

1.   *Sanitary or phytosanitary measure* - Any measure applied:

(a)   to protect animal or plant life or health within the territory of the Member from risks arising from the entry, establishment or spread of pests, diseases, disease-carrying organisms or disease-causing organisms;

(b)   to protect human or animal life or health within the territory of the Member from risks arising from additives, contaminants, toxins or disease-causing organisms in foods, beverages or feedstuffs;

(c)   to protect human life or health within the territory of the Member from risks arising from diseases carried by animals, plants or products thereof, or from the entry, establishment or spread of pests; or

(d)   to prevent or limit other damage within the territory of the Member from the entry, establishment or spread of pests.

Sanitary or phytosanitary measures include all relevant laws, decrees, regulations, requirements and procedures including, *inter alia*, end product criteria; processes and production methods; testing, inspection, certification and approval procedures; quarantine treatments including relevant requirements associated with the transport of animals or plants, or with the materials necessary for their survival during transport; provisions on relevant statistical methods, sampling procedures and methods of risk assessment; and packaging and labelling requirements directly related to food safety.

2.   *Harmonization* - The establishment, recognition and application of common sanitary and phytosanitary measures by different Members.

3.   *International standards, guidelines and recommendations*

(a)   for food safety, the standards, guidelines and recommendations established by the Codex Alimentarius Commission relating to food additives, veterinary drug and pesticide residues, contaminants, methods of analysis and sampling, and codes and guidelines of hygienic practice;

(b)   for animal health and zoonoses, the standards, guidelines and recommendations developed under the auspices of the International Office of Epizootics;

(c)   for plant health, the international standards, guidelines and recommendations developed under the auspices of the Secretariat of the International Plant Protection Convention in cooperation with regional organizations operating within the framework of the International Plant Protection Convention; and

(d) for matters not covered by the above organizations, appropriate standards, guidelines and recommendations promulgated by other relevant international organizations open for membership to all Members, as identified by the Committee.

4. *Risk assessment* - The evaluation of the likelihood of entry, establishment or spread of a pest or disease within the territory of an importing Member according to the sanitary or phytosanitary measures which might be applied, and of the associated potential biological and economic consequences; or the evaluation of the potential for adverse effects on human or animal health arising from the presence of additives, contaminants, toxins or disease-causing organisms in food, beverages or feedstuffs.

5. *Appropriate level of sanitary or phytosanitary protection* - The level of protection deemed appropriate by the Member establishing a sanitary or phytosanitary measure to protect human, animal or plant life or health within its territory.

NOTE: Many Members otherwise refer to this concept as the 'acceptable level of risk'.

6. *Pest- or disease-free area* - An area, whether all of a country, part of a country, or all or parts of several countries, as identified by the competent authorities, in which a specific pest or disease does not occur.

NOTE: A pest- or disease-free area may surround, be surrounded by, or be adjacent to an area - whether within part of a country or in a geographic region which includes parts of or all of several countries -in which a specific pest or disease is known to occur but is subject to regional control measures such as the establishment of protection, surveillance and buffer zones which will confine or eradicate the pest or disease in question.

7. *Area of low pest or disease prevalence* - An area, whether all of a country, part of a country, or all or parts of several countries, as identified by the competent authorities, in which a specific pest or disease occurs at low levels and which is subject to effective surveillance, control or eradication measures.

ANNEX B

TRANSPARENCY OF SANITARY AND PHYTOSANITARY REGULATIONS

Publication of regulations

1. Members shall ensure that all sanitary and phytosanitary regulations which have been adopted are published promptly in such a manner as to enable interested Members to become acquainted with them.

2. Except in urgent circumstances, Members shall allow a reasonable interval between the publication of a sanitary or phytosanitary regulation and its entry into force in order to allow time for producers in exporting Members, and particularly in developing country Members, to adapt their products and methods of production to the requirements of the importing Member.

Enquiry points

3.   Each Member shall ensure that one enquiry point exists which is responsible for the provision of answers to all reasonable questions from interested Members as well as for the provision of relevant documents regarding:

>   (a)   any sanitary or phytosanitary regulations adopted or proposed within its territory;

>   (b)   any control and inspection procedures, production and quarantine treatment, pesticide tolerance and food additive approval procedures, which are operated within its territory;

>   (c)   risk assessment procedures, factors taken into consideration, as well as the determination of the appropriate level of sanitary or phytosanitary protection;

>   (d)   the membership and participation of the Member, or of relevant bodies within its territory, in international and regional sanitary and phytosanitary organizations and systems, as well as in bilateral and multilateral agreements and arrangements within the scope of this Agreement, and the texts of such agreements and arrangements.

4.   Members shall ensure that where copies of documents are requested by interested Members, they are supplied at the same price (if any), apart from the cost of delivery, as to the nationals of the Member concerned.

Notification procedures

5.   Whenever an international standard, guideline or recommendation does not exist or the content of a proposed sanitary or phytosanitary regulation is not substantially the same as the content of an international standard, guideline or recommendation, and if the regulation may have a significant effect on trade of other Members, Members shall:

>   (a)   publish a notice at an early stage in such a manner as to enable interested Members to become acquainted with the proposal to introduce a particular regulation;

>   (b)   notify other Members, through the Secretariat, of the products to be covered by the regulation together with a brief indication of the objective and rationale of the proposed regulation. Such notifications shall take place at an early stage, when amendments can still be introduced and comments taken into account;

>   (c)   provide upon request to other Members copies of the proposed regulation and, whenever possible, identify the parts which in substance deviate from international standards, guidelines or recommendations;

>   (d)   without discrimination, allow reasonable time for other Members to make comments in writing, discuss these comments upon request, and take the comments and the results of the discussions into account.

6.   However, where urgent problems of health protection arise or threaten to arise for a Member, that Member may omit such of the steps enumerated in paragraph 5 of this Annex as it finds necessary, provided that the Member:

(a)   immediately notifies other Members, through the Secretariat, of the particular regulation and the products covered, with a brief indication of the objective and the rationale of the regulation, including the nature of the urgent problem(s);

(b)   provides, upon request, copies of the regulation to other Members;

(c)   allows other Members to make comments in writing, discusses these comments upon request, and takes the comments and the results of the discussions into account.

7.   Notifications to the Secretariat shall be in English, French or Spanish.

8.   Developed country Members shall, if requested by other Members, provide copies of the documents or, in case of voluminous documents, summaries of the documents covered by a specific notification in English, French or Spanish.

9.   The Secretariat shall promptly circulate copies of the notification to all Members and interested international organizations and draw the attention of developing country Members to any notifications relating to products of particular interest to them.

10.   Members shall designate a single central government authority as responsible for the implementation, on the national level, of the provisions concerning notification procedures according to paragraphs 5, 6, 7 and 8 of this Annex.

General reservations

11.   Nothing in this Agreement shall be construed as requiring:

(a)   the provision of particulars or copies of drafts or the publication of texts other than in the language of the Member except as stated in paragraph 8 of this Annex; or

(b)   Members to disclose confidential information which would impede enforcement of sanitary or phytosanitary legislation or which would prejudice the legitimate commercial interests of particular enterprises.

ANNEX C

CONTROL, INSPECTION AND APPROVAL PROCEDURES

1.   Members shall ensure, with respect to any procedure to check and ensure the fulfilment of sanitary or phytosanitary measures, that:

(a)   such procedures are undertaken and completed without undue delay and in no less favourable manner for imported products than for like domestic products;

(b)   the standard processing period of each procedure is published or that the anticipated processing period is communicated to the applicant upon request; when receiving an application, the competent body promptly examines the completeness of the documentation and informs the applicant in a precise and complete manner of all deficiencies; the competent body transmits as soon as possible the results of the procedure in a precise and complete manner to the applicant so that corrective action may be taken if necessary; even when the application has deficiencies, the competent body proceeds as far as practicable with the procedure if the applicant so requests; and that upon request, the applicant is informed of the stage of the procedure, with any delay being explained;

(c)   information requirements are limited to what is necessary for appropriate control, inspection and approval procedures, including for approval of the use of additives or for the establishment of tolerances for contaminants in food, beverages or feedstuffs;

(d)   the confidentiality of information about imported products arising from or supplied in connection with control, inspection and approval is respected in a way no less favourable than for domestic products and in such a manner that legitimate commercial interests are protected;

(e)   any requirements for control, inspection and approval of individual specimens of a product are limited to what is reasonable and necessary;

(f)   any fees imposed for the procedures on imported products are equitable in relation to any fees charged on like domestic products or products originating in any other Member and should be no higher than the actual cost of the service;

(g)   the same criteria should be used in the siting of facilities used in the procedures and the selection of samples of imported products as for domestic products so as to minimize the inconvenience to applicants, importers, exporters or their agents;

(h)   whenever specifications of a product are changed subsequent to its control and inspection in light of the applicable regulations, the procedure for the modified product is limited to what is necessary to determine whether adequate confidence exists that the product still meets the regulations concerned; and

(i)   a procedure exists to review complaints concerning the operation of such procedures and to take corrective action when a complaint is justified.

Where an importing Member operates a system for the approval of the use of food additives or for the establishment of tolerances for contaminants in food, beverages or feedstuffs which prohibits or restricts access to its domestic markets for products based on the absence of an approval, the importing Member shall consider the use of a relevant international standard as the basis for access until a final determination is made.

2.   Where a sanitary or phytosanitary measure specifies control at the level of production, the Member in whose territory the production takes place shall provide the necessary assistance to facilitate such control and the work of the controlling authorities.

3.   Nothing in this Agreement shall prevent Members from carrying out reasonable inspection within their own territories.